Win-Win Competitiveness Made in Canada

How to be Competitive Using the Consensus Approach

by Ben Hoffman

CAPTUS PRESS

Win-Win Competitiveness Made in Canada:
How to be Competitive Using the Consensus Approach

Canadian Cataloguing in Publication Data
Hoffman, Ben, 1950–
    Win-win competitiveness made in Canada :
how to be competitive using the consensus approach

Includes bibliographical references.
ISBN 1-895712-19-X

1. Conflict management — Canada. 2. Competition
— Canada. 3. Negotiation in business — Canada.
4. Consensus (Social sciences). 5. Competition —
Canada. I. Title.

HD42.H64 1993   658   C93-095548-X

Captus Press Inc.
c/o York University Campus
4700 Keele Street
North York, Ontario M3J 1P3
Tel.: (416) 736-5537
Fax: (416) 736-5793

0 9 8 7 6 5 4 3 2 1
Printed in Canada

To my wife, Ann.

Table of Contents

Foreword

"IN *Win-Win Competitiveness Made in Canada*, Ben Hoffman begins by facing the problems we are confronting in Canada today, head-on. Mr. Hoffman declares matter of factly that these problems exceed the abilities of the present system and present practices. The question remains: do we have what it takes to surface, survive and sustain progress in a real sense?

Mr. Hoffman believes we do, and he guides us towards a truly revolutionary approach. This approach is based on the strengths and qualities of the Canadian personality and on strong traditions in Canada. We are encouraged to stick to our values and develop a unique Canadian comparitive advantage. This advantage is one of the keys to our competitiveness in the global economy. It relies on our Canadian tendency to look for consensus—a traditional practice among Canadian aboriginal people and the stuff that has kept this diverse country together from the beginning.

Yes, we have what it takes to pursue Win-Win Competitiveness and I am confident that Mr. Hoffman's vision of the economic advantages of consensus processes will succeed in creating an awareness amongst our people that we have such a potential, and in giving those who wish to act on the idea the tools to start immediately."

Mark Anderson
Editor, *Ottawa Business News*
October, 1993

Acknowledgements

THIS book builds upon the theoretical and practical work of many who have pioneered the field of consensus processes for the past twenty years. Where I am able to give specific credit, I have done so in the Notes. To others who are unnamed but whose influence will be obvious, my thanks as well.

The vision that drives the book can be identified more easily. It all started in a brainstorming session at Concorde Inc. in July, 1991 when Laura Doehring, Colin McKenzie and myself struggled with the demand from our clients to adapt our consensus-building material to meet their needs. They wanted our assistance in employee empowerment, team building and enhanced corporate effectiveness. They wanted to adopt consensus processes to ensure their own survival and success. I can still remember the "eureka" experience when we put cooperation and competition right beside each other and coined the term "win-win competitiveness". Thanks, Laura and Colin.

Others who helped me as I tried to express the working assumptions behind win-win competitiveness and fleshed out the ideas in this book are: Mr. Bhupendra Sharma, Mr. Gerry Pottery, Mr. Brian Barr and Ms. Ann Young. Once again, Laura Doehring was there to work on drafts and her intellectual contributions show up in many of the charts and tables.

At all points my wife Ann provided her critical comments, reviewing the first draft, forcing me to sharpen my focus and supporting me when Sundays and holidays were eroded so that I could write.

This book is dedicated to her.

How This Book is Organized

WIN-WIN *Competitiveness* is based on the consensus approach in human relations and in business. Win-Win approaches enhance personal and organizational health and morale. They contribute to our productivity and effectiveness, and hence, our competitiveness.

This book is organized into five sections:

Section I: Win-Win Competitiveness

‣ Why we need to build on the consensus approach, what Win-Win Competitiveness is and why it is Canadian.

Section II: The Consensus Approach

‣ The power of process: what is the consensus approach, how processes shape outcomes, and examples of using consensus in business and government disputes.

‣ Skills, tools, and systems for success: the essential elements of Win-Win Competitiveness.

Section III: Re-Tooling for Win-Win Competitiveness

‣ You can start anywhere, right where you are. No gurus, no political, religious or cultural program is necessary. You can implement consensus-based approaches in your workplace and in your community now.

Section IV: Win-Win Competitiveness in Canada

‣ Outlines steps that can be taken at the national level to put Canada on the map as the place in which to live and do business.

Section V: Tools to Get Started Now

> ▸ Gives the reader a quick overview of conflict resolution
> and a box of tools so that you can begin now.

The Image of Conflict Resolution

 This image was created by Paul Barron for *Decision-Making in the '90s: The Consensus Approach*, a conference held in Victoria, British Columbia in 1992. Paul's image shows a circle and rectangle balanced on a triangle, with the goal of resolution. The style of the image reflects both Canadian Aboriginal and oriental influences, suggesting the roots of consensus which can be found in these cultures. It also conveys the richness of cultural diversity.

As guest speaker at the conference, I was instantly struck by Paul's logo. In it, I saw my presentation depicted perfectly. To me, the circle represents the **Skills of Conflict Resolution**; the rectangle corresponds to **Systems for Conflict Prevention**; and the triangle stands for the **Tools of Conflict Analysis**, which must be used to achieve the appropriate balance between skills and systems—between resolution of an immediate problem and prevention of future conflicts.

Introduction

MONEY talks.

I recall my father-in-law, Stan Suter, lecturing me on the true reason why so many North Americans were turning to Japanese car imports in the early 70s. While I had been arguing the virtues of fuel conservation as an explanation for the four cylinder car I was then driving, Stan cut me off. "Look", he said "people don't do things that are progressive and responsible because they have seen the light. They do it because the costs of doing otherwise outweigh the benefits."

Stan was certain that higher fuel charges at the tank and police threats to enforce lower speed limits of 55 miles per hour on freeways were the reasons people were driving small imports. They could care less about the environment.

Stan was an educator most of his career, after leaving the government where he had been a forester in the 1950s. He knew and cared about natural resource conservation and he had plenty of experience and a master's degree in education. Nevertheless, a young idealist, I really resisted his cynical analysis.

I was prepared to acknowledge that punishments do shape behaviour; but I have and still do resist approaches to learning that ignore the positive, creative, even inspirational sources of learning and the potential of human beings as they encounter and react to life's challenges.

It is interesting to note that twenty years ago, when Stan and I were having our debate over the motivation for buying a foreign import—(Stan's underlying concern was that his daughter and I had not bought a North American-made car and supported our "own" economy) others were pioneering alternatives of another sort. The greening of America was taking place on a number of fronts.

In the early 70s civil rights and community-development activists were advancing different forms of citizen empowerment and the direct participation of individuals and interest groups in issues and conflicts that affected them. In the United States, the explosion of litigation in a society that really was practising a "you sue me, I'll sue you" form of dispute resolution was also beginning to paralyse the legal system.

Costs and delays in "getting justice" were becoming untenable and alternatives to courts, such as arbitration and mediation were being experimented with. Today a whole range of techniques that support the use of win-win approaches have been developed and are becoming more and more popular for both people in dispute and the professionals who assist them.

The drive toward these consensus-based alternatives, such as negotiation and mediation, are economically motivated in some cases, especially when their cost-effectiveness becomes apparent to governments and officials who are responsible for getting the greatest bang for the public's buck. When the costs of a certain path of action, or a certain program funded by the public purse becomes punitive or unsustainable, we look for alternatives.

In a real sense, Stan was right.

It is true that the use of win-win approaches to find solutions to problems and to deal with disputes across the range of conflicts in society, is cost-effective—and thus their appeal. This is part of the economics of consensus-based approaches, discussed in the chapter on theory and a theme throughout this book.

It is also true that a set of values and principles have been the backbone of those who have pioneered the consensus approach. Whether in dealing with victims and offenders at the community level, where the rubber hits the road in criminal justice, arbitrating a complex business dispute, or mediating at the highest levels of international diplomacy, most proponents and practitioners of the win-win approach have been attempting to do more than serve the economic bottom line.

They have a vision that justice should be accessible to people; that individuals have the ability, with the proper support, to put most things right; that the arbitrary use of authority is unacceptable; that dis-enfranchised individuals and groups must and will have their full participation in life; and that, among others, and perhaps foremost, violence in its many forms is unacceptable.

For these pioneers and advocates of win-win approaches, "money may talk". They may recognize the economic advantages of win-win processes, but that is not what motivates their efforts. Some of them will take issue with this book, concerned that the utilitarian is stressed too much; that consensus processes have been coopted to serve base values, especially a respect for the bottom line.

They will conclude that Win-Win Competitiveness shows that Stan has won the argument with me; that Hobbes was right, man is basically bad. Or, at least, that man is most motivated by fear of punishment and behaviour is most effectively changed by increasing penalties and making the prospects of enforcement certain and swift. Only when the excessive costs of adversarial processes are felt in the pocket book will consensus find its place in mainstream thought and practice.

Win-Win Competitiveness is more than this. Much more, although this book *is* a primer. It is a primer on the *economics* of win-win approaches, and it is a primer on the *economic advantages* of consensus processes. It puts competition and cooperation together. It points us beyond an unproductive debate over growth versus redistribution, laissez-faire versus protectionism, right versus left, private interests versus public goods. It introduces readers to the skills, tools, and systems for success through consensus. It is designed for practical use in business, government, and Canadian communities, now.

As a primer on the *economics* of consensus processes, it attempts to go "inside" the science and dynamics of negotiation-based approaches to problems. In doing so it draws on theory that shows how the tension between the drive to compete and the drive to collaborate can actually produce good outcomes, where good outcomes include economic ones. That is, they are efficient in that *maximum* gains were reached; and they are efficient in that they entail lower transaction costs as compared to adversarial processes.

They are also economic, or cost-effective, inasmuch as win-win outcomes have a tendency to hold up longer. This saves a significant amount of resources that might otherwise be expended in enforcement, and it reduces the likelihood that those involved will have to go back to the drawing board because things have broken down, or as certain parties renege or fail in some way to honour their commitments.

xiii

If they do have to return to the negotiation table, perhaps over a dispute that has arisen during the implementation of an agreement, win-win or consensus processes will generally have anticipated such eventualities; appropriate dispute settlement mechanisms will have been created in advance. Ultimately, the relationship between the parties involved should be sufficiently positive and constructive so that re-visiting problems will be a stress-free experience, not one that needs to be avoided.

As a primer on the *economic advantages* of consensus processes, Win-Win Competitiveness attempts to address human nature and the economics of the business world, head-on. There are secondary economic advantages to negotiation-based, or consensus processes in that they will enhance the competitiveness of those that employ them. That is, in addition to the economies that are "inside" win-win processes and their outcomes, the capacity to perform at optimum levels and to meet the challenges of personal and business life is enhanced.

There is, generally, less "noise in the system" when consensus processes are used and when conflict resolution systems and mechanisms are in place. Creative potential is freed up to be more innovative, to be more productive, and thus to enhance competitiveness.

At the same time, Win-Win Competitiveness, while quite simple and straightforward, is new. New skills, new tools and new systems and processes are necessary to achieve it. My hope is that this book will help those who are looking for a means to establish a greater sense of reliability and hope at a time when we seem to be in the midst of a sea of chaos, when the old is dropping away too quickly, and the new is yet unrevealed.

SECTION I

Win-Win Competitiveness

CHAPTER ONE

The System is Broken— And Old Tools Won't Fix It

CANADA has relied on its natural resources to give us a comparative advantage in the global economy. This is a narrow and self-destructive practice.

We can no longer afford to be a resource-based economy with entire communities clustered around a primary industry. We can no longer be hewers of wood and haulers of water. We must abandon that image. Natural resource-based economies that ship raw materials away for development only to purchase them back again in finished form, exhaust their heritage; they decline and die. We must diversify.

We are on the eve of the 21st century in a post-industrial high technology world where the resources and skills we once relied on can no longer do the job. The systems of wealth production and wealth distribution must change and the mechanisms of competing and collaborating in the course of creating and distributing wealth must also change.

We might wish for a period of stability or a return to days gone by, but the status quo is gone forever. Change, not stability, is a fact of life.

With all this change, we experience conflict. In fact, we are confronting an unprecedented outbreak of open conflict in Canada. So far, there has been little help for us to understand and deal with this challenge—a challenge that we meet at every turn in the road.

The fisheries industry in eastern Canada is on its knees, environmentalists and the forestry industry in western Canada are in conflict. Canada's transportation industry is straining to compete with American firms and many farmers in the prairie provinces have given up hope. The present economic recession seems relentless.

Natives have successfully made the case that they are key stakeholders in this country, wishing to exercise self-determination and forms of self-governance. This has triggered concern in some who either can not understand the aspirations of Aboriginal people or who feel that their own stake in things is being put at risk by Indian claims.

The Canadian Constitutional wranglings were not settled by the referendum in October, 1992 and social strife seems to cascade over us, wave after wave.

This era of conflict is tearing us apart; pulling us in different directions at the same time. We are being pressed to tolerate greater diversity in society and in the workplace. White must get along with Black, developmentally handicapped with gifted, French with English, male with female, straight with gay. Flexibility, understanding, and patience are required. At the same time we are being told that our survival depends on the ability to focus our competitive strengths to meet the challenges of a "new global economic order".

So we are to assert ourselves in ways that we have never done. Yet to assert ourselves, to become competitive is felt by many to be an abandonment of our cherished qualities of "tolerance", and "compromise".

Mixed signals: "be loose", and "be tight"! "Compete", and "cooperate".

Unfortunately, we are analyzing our problems with old concepts, debating issues in old language, and labouring at solutions with old tools. Whether in the factory, the corporate board room, or in the community—we must change to survive.

The system is broken—**and old tools won't fix it.**

CHAPTER TWO

The Objective:
Win-Win Competitiveness

IF we do not change, we can not grow, and if there is no growth, we suffocate. Growth demands a temporary discarding of our security blanket. It may mean relinquishing milestones and the limiting shelter and slogan of "Do not rock the boat". We may have to give up safe but unrewarding work and meaningless relationships. As Dostoevski put it: "Taking a new step, uttering a new word is what people fear most". But this is what is required.

We must set out now to distinguish Canada in the global marketplace by working toward radically improved management-labour relations in the workplace; collaboration between government, labour and the private sector must increase to enhance Canadian competitiveness nationally and internationally; cost-effective procedures and systems for the resolution of business and public disputes must be designed and put into operation; and a strategy for the transformation of our social relations to support a healthy and productive Canadian society is necessary.

To do this, we need to understand, explore and develop our **Win-Win Competitiveness**.

CHAPTER THREE

What is Win-Win Competitiveness?

W IN-WIN Competitiveness is a form of collaborative competition. It is a means of supporting natural competitive instincts through collaborative skills and processes. It emphasizes negotiated solutions over all other means of seeking solutions to problems and of managing conflict. Win-win approaches result in increased efficiency. Less personal, organizational and societal energy is expended in dealing with differences and in producing solutions to problems; and the solutions found, the products of our relationships and transactions are superior. Our competitiveness is enhanced.

Win-Win Competitiveness is a practical approach to problems based on attitudes, skills, and systems which reconcile, in a realistic and productive way, the drive to compete and the drive to cooperate. Both of which are felt simultaneously in most of life's situations.

Win-Win Competitiveness, applied, takes us beyond the dilemma of having to choose compromise, on the one hand, or coercion, on the other. Compromise can result in the lowest common denominator—an unacceptable outcome for winners. Coercion relies on power tactics—and no one wants to be the loser in a struggle for dominance. Win-Win Competitiveness is the constructive management of differences, and offers us more than compromise through concession or "victory" through force.

Win-Win Competitiveness asserts that decisions and actions that are based on choosing a competitive mode or a cooperative mode to the exclusion of the other are counterproductive. Our complex world demands both competitive and cooperative initiatives, often at the same time.

In personal and in business relations it is necessary to adopt negotiation-based approaches that will generate win-win solutions to problems, cost-effectively. In doing so we are able to enhance our health, our productivity, and our competitiveness.

Win-Win Competitiveness takes a new turn, and is based on the notion of survival of the finest. Together, we "squeeze the lemon".

DIRECT APPLICATIONS OF WIN-WIN COMPETITIVENESS:

‣ improved management-labour relations;

‣ collaboration between government, the private sector and labour to build financial, regulatory, and wealth production and distribution systems which increase Canadian competitiveness nationally and internationally;

‣ provisions for resolving commercial business disputes and public policy disputes cost-effectively; and

‣ the long-term transformation of social relations through education, personal and professional development, and community renewal.

↓

DIRECT BENEFITS:

‣ creative solutions to problems
‣ improved individual and organizational health
‣ improved productivity
‣ reduced costs
‣ enhanced competitiveness
‣ sustainable development

CHAPTER FOUR

The Theory of Win-Win Competitiveness

WE hear the phrase "win-win" is heard more often all the time. "Negotiation" is in the news every day.

Given the fact that we live in a state of relative peace, it is reasonable to say that most of our problems are solved by negotiation of some sort. We "negotiate" life.

"Competitiveness" has also become a buzz-word for the nineties. How, we might ask, can competitiveness be joined with the idea of negotiating win-win solutions? If we both win, how can that be competitive?

First, the win-win approach is based on the view that few conflicts are really structured in a way the one side must "win" and the other "lose".[1]

The win-lose notion, in contrast, is based on the view that a conflict situation is "zero-sum": a "plus 1" for me, and a "minus 1" for you equals zero. One of us will win, the other lose. And the game "zeroes" out.

The zero-sum, win-lose view of life tends to treat every situation as though there is a fixed pie that is being struggled over, and a larger piece for me will obviously mean a smaller piece for you. Unfortunately, this is the way our legal system is set up, the way our management-employee relations are structured, and the way our political system operates. A judge decides a winner and a loser; labour and management fight with the weapons of the "strike" or the "lock out"; and individual politicians are forced to serve their political party's struggle for victory where a vote of 51 to 49 will decide the matter.

When we see the world as a fixed pie, the psychology of scarcity dominates. It breeds fear, it makes power the critical ingredient for success and it produces systems to regulate the struggle which always ends with a winner and a loser.

An alternative approach is possible.

That is the consensus approach. Solutions to problems are sought through negotiation. The negotiated solution is the point of consensus. Win-win is the objective. And win-win is possible, for a number of reasons.

It is common to equate the win-win approach with compromise. Canadians have always sought the "honourable compromise". In some respects we have been able to hold this large and culturally diverse country together through compromise. Compromise, however, has its limits; there are some things of importance to people that simply will not be traded away.

Win-Win Competitiveness relies on more than compromise.

Win-Win Competitiveness recognizes and builds upon the fact that the potential to create innovative solutions to disputes is not necessarily based on compromise. It is possible for one side to "win" on a particular matter of interest to them without the other side experiencing a "loss". These win-win solutions can be developed up to a "frontier of possibilities" wherein joint gain can be realized and beyond which a "win" for one side will be perceived as a "loss" for the other (see figure).

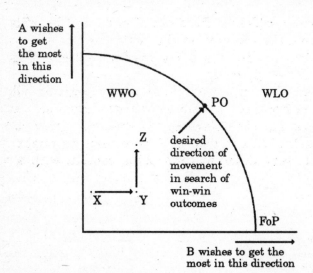

X = A possible outcome; the least rich, the fewest joint gains (A sells house to B for $150,000).

Y = A richer outcome; B gets more at no perceived loss to A (A changes closing date to convenience B).

Z = A richer outcome yet; A gets more at no perceived loss to B (B stores A's furniture in unused garage to save A costs while redecorating new home).

FoP = Frontier of Possibilities: the point up to which win-win solutions are possible; based on Pareto's theory of optimality.

PO   = Some point on the frontier of possibilities where the agreement or solution reached by A and B are "Pareto Optimal"; maximum joint gains are realized.

WWO = Area wherein both A and B are able to make trades and generate creative solutions that are perceived as a win for each; maximum joint gain possible.

WLO = Area wherein an objective achieved by one will result in a perceived loss by the other.

To achieve our objectives in life, to surpass the threshold of mere survival, and to excel in our efforts to develop and realize the product of all our potential, we must do better than compromise. We must set out to get more than the lowest common denominator—and that is all that a compromise often achieves. More is possible.

How?

We can take advantage of the fact that in most disputes different parties give different priority to different interests. The ability to trade across these differences is one of the keys to achieving satisfactory outcomes. It is based on the clear articulation of each party's interests, the acknowledgement that there is seldom a fixed set of costs and benefits in any dispute, and the recognition that what may be a requirement (a high priority) for one party may not disadvantage (incur costs to) the other party.

We can also build on the creative powers of individuals who are confronting a problem. With good communication and problem-solving skills, synergy is possible. Creative tension and collaboration can generate more than we might expect.

This is very different than being content with a compromise agreement reached through the trading of concessions. It is, rather, a matter of capitalizing on the differences of the parties in dispute.

> The story is told about two sisters arguing over the last orange in the refrigerator. Both want the orange and rather than sorting out what it is they need it for, they argue instead. Each declares, "It's mine, I want it." After fighting over the orange, they agree to cut it in half, a compromise solution. One sister peels half, throws the peel away, and eats the pulp; the other peels her half, throws the inside away and grates the peel to use in a recipe for icing a cake she has baked.

> This simple story demonstrates so many things that are wrong with approaches to disputes that fail to get the parties talking so that they can discover what their real interests are. Both sisters could have got what they wanted, and a whole orange full at that, had they got past a win-lose approach and on to a win-win outcome. The story also shows how a compromise settlement really can be a second best outcome, warning us that compromise as an approach to disputes is far less than optimal.

Those of us who have a worldview of fixed and scarce resources, over which parties compete in a zero-sum game naturally develop a personal approach to life and to business relations that gives rise to strong adversarial behaviour. That produces a world of winners and losers. And those who have enjoyed access to and use of resources—the winners—very naturally have built systems designed to protect their self-interest.

The problem of course, is that we all want to be winners. And furthermore, as the increase in open conflict shows, individuals and groups that believe they have a stake in matters of importance to them are insisting on getting their share of the pie.

Winning by coercing, overpowering and oppressing the other side is not an enduring solution. Compromise, as we have seen and as many of us have probably personally experienced, is often less than satisfactory in the long run. Moreover, the idea of trading concessions is hardly an optimal "win-win" strategy. That is, I agree to give up this item which is important to me if you agree to give up that item which is important to you, eventually leading us to a sub-optimal outcome. It may "feel" like we have both won, but it doesn't meet the standard of getting as many joint gains from the negotiation as possible. Maximum joint gains are found by pushing toward the frontier of win-win possibilities.

Conflict management that relies on either coercion or compromise is a limited repertoire with considerable costs. Yet many people and most political arrangements rely on these approaches, in part because realistic alternatives seem to be in short supply or inadequate to meet the challenges of the day.

Developments in ecology and the social sciences, however, support the idea of Win-Win Competitiveness.[2] Joint gains are possible in most circumstances. Survival of both parties depends on creative abilities to find integrative, non-zero sum solutions to problems of resource distribution and co-existence. Cooperation is in fact more the rule than the exception in nature. Yet our competitive instincts are just as real.

The win-win approach, and its practical applications in daily life, includes better ways of expressing anger and solving interpersonal conflicts and business disputes, as well as stimulating new forms of production and political organization.

Win-Win has taken most of the Twentieth Century just to find its footing. Win-Win Competitiveness brings it into mainstream thought.

Win-Win Competitiveness is not just an interesting term that combines apparently contradictory notions. One of the most useful ways to judge Win-Win Competitiveness is to put it to use, and then measure its effectiveness.

Practical experience says it works. It works in interpersonal conflicts, in team efforts to work together and to achieve maximum productivity, in settling commercial and corporate disputes, and in resolving contentious public policy issues, such as resource management.

For a systematic test, there are four criteria which can be used to measure a "good" outcome to a dispute. An agreement reached through win-win approaches can be tested against the criteria of whether it is Fair, Wise, Efficient, and Enduring.[3]

FAIRNESS will be assessed by each party to the dispute. While the sense that something is "fair" will be based on considerations of the merits of the case as put forward by both sides, taking into account any industry standards or objective criteria for evaluating a claim or proposal, fairness is typically a subjective measure. Each party must assess whether the outcome was fair, and a "good" outcome has been shown to be one that is fair to all concerned.

The **WISDOM** of an agreement refers to how it would be perceived with perfect hindsight, many years hence. Would the parties who have negotiated the agreement look back and be able to conclude that they had shown wisdom in their negotiation? For example, were the interests of third parties considered; were changing conditions and contingencies accounted for? Were things taken into account that might never

11

have been considered if the negotiators hadn't paid particular attention to fashioning a wise agreement?

The test of **EFFICIENCY** has two dimensions to it. Efficiency applies to the ease with which a settlement is reached and the degree to which the settlement includes the maximum amount of joint gain possible. The transaction costs are thus a consideration, and so to is the matter of "how much juice" the negotiators were able to extract from the potential that both parties brought to the table. The objective is to get as rich an agreement as possible within reasonable transaction costs.

An **ENDURING** agreement is one that will stand the test of time. Commitments made are honoured and implementation problems are resolved through mechanisms set in place at the time of negotiating the agreement. If the agreement is fair, wise, and efficient, it will likely endure.

These four criteria, taken together and applied in a balanced way against the outcome of a given dispute or conflict are the means of measuring or testing the value of a particular approach to a problem.

The win-win approach has thus been advanced by some of its advocates on the basis of its cost-effectiveness. *It is estimated that one dollar spent on mediation will cost three for arbitration and fifteen for litigation. Consensus-based processes are proving to be cost effective.*

Furthermore, win-win approaches recognize and address the competitive agenda of parties in a dispute. Since consensus-based approaches are more efficient—they produce richer outcomes at lower transactions costs—they contribute to the competitiveness agenda of those who employ them. That is, they reconcile the inherent tension between competitive and cooperative drives in the actual negotiation or problem-solving situation, and they generate "good" outcomes at less cost than conventional win-lose, purely adversarial approaches. For example, a business dispute that is settled in a fraction of the time at a significantly lower cost not only is attractive in its own right but leaves more energy and resources to be directed in the productive activities of wealth creation and distribution.

Disputes and conflicts will occur. They are inevitable. They are even desirable if progress is to occur.

Parties in dispute or conflict generally have interests that they share in common, as well as those that are opposed.

Dispute resolution processes that are designed and managed in a manner to produce fair, wise, and efficient outcomes will likely also produce outcomes that will endure. The process of negotiation, including forms of "assisted negotiation" such as mediation, can be cost-effective in reducing the transaction costs normally associated with the adversarial system of dispute resolution. Negotiation can also create an opportunity for the parties to jointly "squeeze the lemon", so that both come away with a sense of having won, and not merely through the trading of concessions.

Critics of win-win approaches have argued that consensus-based processes fail to recognize and make provision for the legitimate self-interests of people in dispute. They claim that "win-win" relies on a set of attitudes and human relations skills that are unrealistic—even wimpish. As such, how could a win-win approach form a central element in anyone's approach to life? How could win-win sustain anyone in the tough world of business?

The fact is that there are three principal elements at issue in most disputes—rights, interests, and power. None of these is ignored in processes based on the win-win approach. Provisions in win-win dispute settlement procedures, such as mediation, do exist to accommodate rights, interests, and power. They are accommodated, however, in a non-adversarial, resolution-seeking context. Critical skills include communication, negotiation, and problem-solving with an emphasis on the art and science of persuasion.

Win-win approaches are not "soft" or "wimpy" alternatives to adversarial approaches. Disputing parties who choose alternative forms of conflict resolution such as conciliation, mediation, and other varieties of assisted negotiation do articulate their legitimate interests, often forcefully. They are supported in doing so.

Obviously, parties in conflict who elect to use a win-win approach to manage the conflict still perceive some of their interests as incompatible with those held by the other side. Negotiated solutions can be difficult to find. They take great skill, understanding, and creativity.

In the most entrenched dispute, the strongest efforts using a win-win approach may realistically only yield an agreement to disagree, and a set of measures by which the parties can live with their differences.

13

Even this is a major improvement on the conventional approach which would produce either one winner, and one loser—or more likely, two losers.

These are some of the theoretical roots of the "Win-Win" part of Win-Win Competitiveness.

In and of themselves, they are not "Canadian". They are generally, in their intellectual origin, American. American scholars have explored, developed and given the clearest expression to them. They have clarified the strategic and economic features of win-win approaches.[4]

Ironically, when you think of competition and "competitiveness", you will most likely also think "American".[5]

It is in Canada, however, that "win-win" can be combined with "competitiveness"; we can innovate while remaining true to our nature. This can be done by explicitly setting out to reconcile these two apparently contradictory notions. Just as the Japanese take materials, ideas, and products and improve on them, so Canada can innovate on an idea, a social technology found in "win-win", and a fundamental dimension of life, "competitiveness".[6]

CHAPTER FIVE

But in Canada?

CANADIANS, it might still be argued, are simply not competitive types. Why should we fall into the "competitiveness trap"? Why should we buy "being competitive"?

Win-Win Competitiveness is based on the view that unfettered competition is not healthy; it is recognized, in fact, that very little if any competition in any civilized society is unfettered. It is only when the rule of law has broken down that the rule of force prevails. When force prevails competition is unfettered, or perhaps more accurately stated, competitive drives are thus aided by gunpower.

The use of force in the service of predatory goals is clearly unacceptable. Furthermore, aggressive and predatory behaviour are actually different: aggression itself does not result in the elimination of species in the animal kingdom, and forms of regulated competition, or managed conflict, are commonplace in human affairs. Even in wars, which are zero-sum, the parties in conflict agree and generally adhere to a set of rules governing the struggle for victory.

Finally, assertiveness is different from aggressiveness, and the ability to assert one's legitimate self-interest is essential. Win-win approaches do not compromise that ability.

The fact is, we cooperate to compete. Some of the most successful competitors in business insist that they welcome quality competition. Good competition ensures high standards of productivity and product quality, distinguishing certain players in the marketplace and discouraging others whose performance contributes to inefficiencies, unrealistic pricing and gluts; and worse, the wholesale discrediting of a product or service. A creative, healthy tension usually exists between competitors; and competitors often form alliances and associations to achieve their common objectives.

It is clear that the Canadian government has been driving toward a re-structuring of the Canadian economy with a goal

15

to make us more competitive internationally. Unfortunately, the economic philosophy has generally followed American thinking and American models. A *Canadian* approach has not been articulated.

Canada's history in labour relations, however, and our idea of the individual and society, and our national characteristic of favouring accommodation, cause a negative knee-jerk reaction when we hear the words "compete", or "competitiveness".

There is no question that the survival of the social programs and the quality of life we have come to expect is related to our ability to participate at an economically viable level in the world. We must create the wealth we wish to distribute among ourselves.

We are also told: "Canadians can compete!" The evidence with respect to our productivity, our capacity to be a trading nation, and our prospects for economic growth suggests this is true.

It is in the Canadian psyche to stand tall for what we believe in, to fight for just causes, and to rise to the occasion when we are in direct conflict. We are duly proud of what our soldiers have been able to accomplish against great odds on the battlefield. We are willing to compete for what we believe in.

This side of our national character is usually understated but it is not to be ignored or undervalued when we examine who we are, and how we will choose to express ourselves in the international context, including our participation in the global economy.

It is the *form of competitiveness* that may be at issue for those Canadians who are uncomfortable with "competition". It is the suggestion that we must become something other than who we are that is disturbing. We refuse to believe in and support a society driven by an emphasis on the pursuit of individual gratifications through win-lose, cut-throat competitive behaviour.

Nevertheless, Canadians are responding to the fact that efficiency is an advantage and that excellence will be rewarded. We are comfortable with certain aspects of competition and we have our own sense of what form of competitiveness is worth pursuing.

The "competitiveness" part of "win-win competitiveness" is rooted in Canadians. It is a human drive; we are survivors.

We can develop a new comparative advantage in building a Canadian capacity for Win-Win Competitiveness. Just as the comparative advantage of some nations, such as Japan, Germany and Switzerland is an extension of their peoples' national character, so too can Canadians draw on our national character to distinguish us in the international global economy, without compromise to our values.

CHAPTER SIX

Yes!
A Made-in-Canada Approach

WIN-WIN Competitiveness requires new attitudes and skills, particularly in negotiating, problem-solving, and in the organization of work and production. These are necessary to rise above strictly adversarial-based approaches to relationships and problems. A "made in Canada" approach is necessary in order to enhance the opportunities for greater productivity, greater individual and group responsiveness to challenges, and greater success of individuals, the group, or the business enterprise.

In an organizational context, strictly adversarial approaches to management-employee relations or, externally, to other organizations (even competitors) fail to realize the advantages to be found in the constructive management of the tension between competitive drives and cooperative/collaborative approaches.

At the practical business level this can be seen in internal matters with respect to employee-employee relationships including conflict on the job, in marketing, in sales and the closing of contracts, in the external relations of the firm with suppliers and clients, and even in the collaboration among competitor firms in the form of strategic alliances, joint ventures, and mergers to ensure productivity, effectiveness, and survival.

Organizations, whether private or public, are thus confronted with training, professional development, and educational awareness issues; with operational and procedural issues; and with some very challenging implementation issues if they wish to build a capacity for Win-Win Competitiveness.

As already discovered in certain experiments and innovations in Canada, however, the direct importation of management philosophy and methods from Japan or Germany will not work. Adaptation to the Canadian scene, which includes

18

Canadian management-labour relations, Canadian government regulations, the Canadian worker's values and psychology, Canadian financial infrastructure and tax structure, and even Canadian physical conditions such as great distances and weather extremes all must be taken into account when searching for answers.

That is not all. That might be enough if we were dealing with a conventional recession and working our way out of a slump to another upturn. In an otherwise "normal" situation our best efforts to adopt and modify models from Germany and Japan might be adequate. As the evidence in the Canadian manufacturing sector shows, however, the underlying and more significant fact is that a virtual re-structuring is taking place. *Something invented in Canada is called for.*

An August, 1992 editorial in The Financial Post makes this point dramatically, declaring in its headline: *Restructuring puts us in new ball game.*[7]

"The "R" word that afflicts markets and economies these days is not the Recession but Restructuring.

A massive correction worldwide is underway. If this was a traditional recession, low inflation and low interest rates would have sparked a dramatic recovery by now. That hasn't happened as yet and do not count on it for a while.

That's because this, as a sportscaster would lament, is a brand new ball game. And most players don't know the new rules or how to win in this decade."

The answers offered? First, "flee to quality". Second, Canadian leaders and managers are to adopt a strategy of making sure the playing "field is in good shape, the tickets are priced properly, the bullpen is full of talent and everyone attends batting practice."

This is why Canada can make win-win competitiveness its comparative advantage.

Let's deal first with quality.

The Post's editorial states that "Markets will reward companies and individuals who make excellent widgets, or provide first-class services, and make profits.

That means for the first time in decades, only smarts and/or effort will equal success. It could mean better mousetraps, real wealth creation, technological breakthroughs and decent multiples for growth stocks."

Win-Win Competitiveness is the basis for unleashing the creative potential of individuals and enterprises so that smarts and efforts are unobstructed in the pursuit of quality. Improved individual and organizational capabilities for finding solutions to problems at the research and development stage, in production, and in marketing and sales are required in the environment of the nineties and the new world economic order.

But these will not be enough. *The entire context in which such efforts are expended will need to be improved.* This is the second point in the Post's editorial.

"For Canadian leaders and managers, the *only* strategy is to make sure the field is in good shape, the tickets priced properly, the bullpen is full of talent and everyone attends batting practice.

Our educational system, our skills development and upgrading techniques, our regulatory framework, and our monetary policy will need to be fine tuned to give Canada the best possible comparative advantage. Can we really do this?"

The editorial goes on: "Canada is too small to change economic events. So is everyone else, including even the U.S. Free trade and global borrowing have made everyone co-dependent which means negative events in Germany and Japan whipsaw our economy or the American one as severely as does the disappearance of cod in Newfoundland or the oil depression in Houston."

The answer? "So as the correction continues, investors and players must cast around for quality. *That's because this is no recession. This is a whole new ball game.*"

Canada can distinguish itself in this new ball game by developing a capacity for competitiveness that is a win-win competitiveness. This includes an economic framework that keeps the field in good shape by having businesses ready and capable of producing quality, free of the costs and destructive elements of poorly managed conflicts between co-workers and between management and labour; by ensuring that Canada is not only seen to be "open for business" but that Canada is a special place in which to do business, a place where energies are released and expended efficiently, where regulatory, financial and legal systems and procedures actually facilitate these goals.

We are long past being able to rely on our natural resources to give us a comparative advantage in the global economy. Even our most productive industries face stiff competition in the global marketplace. Canadian business cannot afford to be passive or reactive. Nor can we hope to be pulled out of our troubles by the Americans. We may find some short-term relief by piggy-backing on the Americans. It is now time, and we have the essential ingredients, to build our capacity for a Win-Win Competitiveness, made-in-Canada.

Information, knowledge, and skills are what will separate the successes from the failures—our human resources—our people—are our greatest resource.

George Peapples, President, General Motors of Canada agrees:

> Only proper cultivation of human resources can give business a sustained competitive advantage. Management must understand that workers at any job can make a significant contribution and they must provide opportunities for their workers to make that contribution.
>
> Management's task is quite clear: it must create a culture where people are given the opportunity to contribute and to question what they are doing. Management can take three positive steps to nurture this questioning attitude.[8]
>
> First, it must recognize that the most knowledgable person about any job is the individual who is actually performing the task. Second, it must encourage workers to use all their talents. Third, management must accept the not so radical theory that business thrives with effort from the bottom and support and leadership from the top.
>
> These steps include a solid commitment of management and the employee to education and training. A knowledgeable, well-trained work force is vital to the success of business, especially a work force that accepts new challenges, welcomes change and can learn new skills.

Gordon Simpson, writing in the Globe and Mail in February, 1991, insists that training is Canada's competitive edge, but points to the essential role of management.[9]

> It is, after all management that provides the vital link between improved worker skills and increased productivity and superior products. The best-trained workers,

21

using the most advanced technology, cannot make Canada competitive if management fails to do its job.

Today, that job has changed or is changing. The management skills that sufficed in the past are not adequate to meet the challenges of the 90s. The old hierarchical system of management is becoming increasingly obsolete. The old system of allowing problems to filter up from the shop floor or front-line sales force, through multiple layers of management, until they come to the attention of the people with the power to make decisions is just too slow to bring success in today's world.

Workplace partnerships and employee empowerment that unleash the thinking and problem-solving abilities of shop floor and front-line employees open the way to success in the 90s.

New approaches, new skills, and new systems are necessary in the areas of management, the organization of work, in production, marketing, sales *and* in dispute resolution.

Some of these are being explored and adopted by companies in the private sector and organizations in the public service where "necessity" is serving as the "mother of invention."

But more needs to be done to develop our *new* comparative advantage.

SECTION II

The Consensus Approach

CHAPTER SEVEN

The Power of Process

I have argued that when two or more minds meet, conflict exists. Conflict occurs the moment anyone perceives their interests to be incompatible with other's. Furthermore, I can't imagine two people meeting and being together for any amount of time without finding themselves in conflict.

Conflict itself, as we must now recognize, is normal. It is a sign of individual differences and the perception that what I want is somehow incompatible with what you want. So we clash. Too many unresolved conflicts will eventually bog down our relationship, or a single major dispute can also lead to impasse.

I have also argued that people in conflict can use various forms of conflict "management" to settle a dispute. These include avoidance, withdrawal, coercion and violence; or, negotiation. Of the lot, negotiation is the best means to seek a solution to a problem people have or to resolve a dispute.

To negotiate is to take the consensus approach.

The agreement that is negotiated, no matter how small or serious the conflict, is the point of consensus. It is the common ground that the parties in dispute have found. This common ground, whether a compromise solution or a creative pooling of their minds to find what we call a "rich" agreement, is the point of resolution upon which they can move forward.

The problem is that most of the processes of communication and the way we organize ourselves to solve problems and settle disputes makes resolution difficult at best, impossible at worst.

This is a serious and critically important point.

Canadian communications theorist Marshall McLuhan revolutionized much of our thinking about communication. He asserted "the medium is the message"; we must recognize another fundamental truth: *there is power in process.*

The consensus approach is based on specific *processes* of human interaction, communication, and problem-solving.

For centuries we have relied upon the British "adversarial" system, believing it to be the best method of sorting out differences, seeking the truth, and settling matters in dispute. Its virtues are that it sets out to remove vengeance from the justice system, to protect the rights of accused people, making a presumption of innocence until they are proven guilty. It is, however, a system closely tied to rewards and punishments.

Many critics of the adversarial system—including those who practice the Law within it—will agree that its procedures and safeguards intended to support the truth and underpin justice are often obstacles to the truth and loopholes for avoiding responsibility.

There is no question, however, that the adversarial system dominates our society—running through it from the way we set up authoritarian relationships to the procedures of collective bargaining between labour and management to the formality of the courtroom. This system has evolved as one means of managing conflict.

Other *processes* for getting along together and for dealing with tough issues and deeply felt conflict do exist. One is the consensus approach.

But what is consensus? The word is often talked about, and idealized as a panacea for our troubles. We hear that government negotiators are "seeking consensus", thus making the word rather commonplace. Yet consensus itself is seldom defined. Few people actually practice it or even experiment with it.

For many of us, the *process of consensus* seems foreign. Images are conjured up of Canadian Indians siting around in circles, discussing matters for days on end, unable to come to a decision, and to take swift action.

The process of consensus is often criticized as too cumbersome, too slow.

Consensus processes, it is argued, may be suited to another time or place. Perhaps to a pre-industrial village where everyone knew each other and had the time to talk things through. Consensus might be suited to a closely knit Quaker community, to other Eastern cultures—but certainly not to a modern Canadian city or a business fighting for survival in today's competitive economy.

The fact of the matter, as discussed elsewhere in this book, is that consensus processes are finding their way into mainstream society precisely because the adversarial system and its techniques are nearly bankrupt. In addition to the excessive economic costs associated with the adversarial system is the unmet human need that is calling out for satisfaction. People want better ways of living together and better ways of sorting out their problems.

There are a number of definitions of consensus, and there have been attempts made to rank, or order, the "levels" of consensus.

Consensus has been defined as "unanimous agreement", "the spirit of a meeting", or in some cases consensus is said to exist when no one involved raises an objection to the solution found or decision reached. Practical people might say consensus is reached when everyone involved is able to say "I can live with that".

The outcomes reached through consensus, however, are distinguished by a singular feature. No one imposes the solution on anyone. The solution to the problem, or the settlement reached in a conflict is arrived at by the parties involved. They have the final say over what they will accept. The meeting of minds, the common ground, the settlement is—in the end—given legitimacy and power by the people directly involved.

This is very different than a settlement that is imposed on people. The process of consensus is fundamentally different than the adversarial process when the adversarial process implies an imposed settlement.

I expect, furthermore, that the *quality* of an imposed settlement is different than one reached through consensus. Even when the parties in a dispute agree to live by the decision of a judge, the quality of the judge's decision will be different than one arrived at by the people directly involved.

I recognize that in some cases this may be the only realistic thing to do—to give the decision-making power over to a third party. But the process of disputing and seeking resolution is different and the outcome, I contend, will not have the qualities of one that is reached through consensus. If the win-win approach is used and the agreement reflects the maximum amount of joint gain possible, it will be richer.

This brings us to the process of consensus—and the power of process.

Adversarial processes are used to deliver solutions imposed by a third party, often a judge—someone in authority. Adversarial processes are associated with adversarial techniques such as debate and forms of argument that set out to negate, knock down, make irrelevant, obstruct and destroy the credibility of one side's "position" "case" or "appeal".

Adversarial processes and techniques of communication do little for building or restoring healthy interpersonal or business relationships; they do not promote creative solutions; they cost too much in human and economic terms.

Yet despite these criticisms, advocates of adversarial processes will point out that many disputes that fall to the adversarial system are settled by negotiation and comparatively few go to a judge or adjudicator. The problem is that the adversarial process militates against resolution rather than facilitates it.

The power of process comes to light when we recognize that people and groups who perceive themselves to have incompatible interests—people in conflict—have a certain constraint set on them by the very processes they use to resolve their differences.

In practical business terms, if adversarial processes are used, we arrive once again at lost efficiency, anger, and acrimony setting in between opposing groups. Efforts to settle matters are costly, and the outcomes are usually uncreative and can be unworkable solutions to the problem. Better processes must be found.

What, then, is the consensus process? How would it apply in government and in business?

The best illustrations may come from descriptions of work we have done in actual cases. We have used consensus processes to help build high-performing teams and to work through a company's mission statement and strategic plan. We have also used consensus processes successfully in tough conflicts ranging from disputes among the shareholders of a large international consulting company to a reconciliation agreement reached between victims of child abuse and the institutions responsible for their care.

Before illustrating the power and applicability of consensus processes, it is helpful to list some of the typical features of this approach.

Consensus processes typically:

- are *voluntary*
- are *informal*
- begin with the setting of *"ground rules"*—including how the discussions will be held and what is open for discussion (in setting ground rules the objective of solving problems rather than blaming others is established, human courtesies, such as not interrupting the person who is speaking are agreed to, what will constitute agreement—i.e., unanimity or majority vote—is clarified, and often the parties in dispute are reminded to keep their past and future relationship in mind as they work through the conflict)
- are *facilitated* or *mediated* by a trusted, impartial third party whose skills are such that he/she can assist the negotiation or problem solving
- rely on the parties to *jointly obtain information* upon which decisions will be made
- are *structured "in the round"* rather than one side set across the table from the other with a judge in the middle, or elevated on a platform
- are *flexible*, such that the parties express what issues are important to them, and then together establish the order of the agenda
- promote the disclosure of the human side of matters in dispute, including the needs, wants, fears and concerns of the people involved rather than debating the positions held or sought
- encourage a respect for differences rather than assimilation or dominance
- generate decisions that are "owned" by the people involved

What is unique about the consensus approach is that it relies on a process that appears to put everything at risk in order to obtain something that is secure. Unlike strategic planning processes and other approaches that tend to control the agenda and structure the flow of information and the communication between key players, the consensus approach starts with the people in dispute.

Consensus processes empower the disputants to express their deepest concerns in a forum that creates enough safety, or levels of security, so that the humanly felt conflict which underlies the dispute is expressed.

The consensus process typically has five overlapping stages that have been identified as:

1. opening statements, wherein the parties, with the assistance and support of a "neutral" facilitator or mediator, express their positions, and perhaps state their objectives with respect to the dispute or issue around which consensus is being sought.
2. the *underlying issues are identified*, often by the "neutral" and the parties jointly organize these into an agenda.
3. the *issues are explored* in an informal give and take, ideally through direct face-to-face discussions between the parties involved and with the help, but not "through" the neutral.
4. solutions to the problems that have been expressed, including the needs and concerns of the parties that are embedded in or at the seat of the conflict *are worked out*, using problem solving techniques and negotiation.
5. agreements are reached, and commitments are made with respect to any actions necessary to implement the agreement.

This type of process is foreign to litigators, to the arbitrator, and even to the professional planner. The litigator and arbitrator are accustomed to strictly controlled "representations" from the parties, the presentation of "evidence" in defence of a case or as a means of attacking the credibility of the other side's position, cross examination, and then adjudication by a judge.

Strategic planners will recognize their process as a form of "gap" analysis, with a view to filling in the gap. The "vision" of where a group or corporation wishes to be is established as the first step. This is followed by techniques to encounter where the group or corporation is presently at. The "gap" between the "ideal" and the "real" is thus clarified, and objectives, strategies and tactics for achieving the overall goal are enumerated to bridge the gap.

Consensus processes make no assumptions about shared visions or common objectives. At best, an assumption is made that the parties are prepared to try negotiation as a means of reaching a resolution, but that any one or all of them may walk away at any time.

This sets up a dynamic tension that helps ensure the integrity of any settlement that is reached. The negotiated agreement has to meet some minimum standard of acceptability for each person involved. Achieving or surpassing that standard ensures the integrity of the settlement.

The consensus process puts the parties at the centre of their dispute and those who assist them are responsible for managing the process, but they do not impose solutions. This implies a certain amount of risk for the individuals involved.

The degree of risk taking inherent in consensus processes is a consideration that is compounded by the concern one might have about the ability of the parties to act on their own behalf. Clearly, some people would prefer to send their representative to do their negotiating for them; others would simply have their day in court. For them, a judge's decision will satisfy. Or, whatever the boss says is OK.

Consensus processes, however, really do empower the people directly involved in the issue. They find that they are able to get their underlying concerns on the table, they have much more control over a process that is people-centred rather than procedure-centred. If they are able to negotiate effectively they arrive at rich, creative outcomes that they are more likely to honour because they had a hand in crafting them.

Take Bacma International as an example. This international consulting company had forty practitioners working in two of Canada's major cities, a leader in its field of specialization.

Despite a long and successful financial track record Bacma was facing major difficulties when one of its senior practitioners called our company for help.

Exhausted with internal wrangling, financially stressed by the recession which began in 1991, overburdened with high fixed operating costs, paralysed at the board level so that no decisions had been made for months, and on the verge of director and employee mutiny, we used a mediation model to assist this company to recover.

First: private, confidential interviews were held with each of the directors, who recognized that our involvement was as mediators, not as management consultants or as corporate lawyers—although we knew that management consulting and corporate law would have a place in our intervention.

The problems identified in these interviews were almost overwhelming when taken together. The list included:

‣ low trust levels among the directors

‣ the President's management style
‣ an accumulated deficit/unsatisfied obligations to directors and to the corporation, in the amount of $750,000
‣ lack of synergy necessary to exploit strengths of the firm's consultants
‣ poor decisions, dysfunctional decision-making practices
‣ a corporate practice of conflict avoidance and resentfulness
‣ a strategic alliance with two other corporations unresolved and external relations becoming acrimonious as outside firms grew impatient
‣ perceived inequities in the distribution of profits
‣ high stress levels in some directors, causing illness
‣ personality clashes at junior levels that remained unaddressed and infectious
‣ no plans for succession at senior levels
‣ self-interest dominating commitments to the company, influencing billing practices and the spawning of smaller companies within the overall structure
‣ different and competing corporate cultures in divisions within the corporation
‣ executive control centres and processes not resolved
‣ inability to attract and retain potential investors/consultants

After examining this list we wondered whether there was any hope for the company!

More immediately we worried whether a consensus approach using a mediation model would work. The overwhelming temptation was to ask for a mandate to cut through all of the problems, to issue edicts, fire and hire staff, and re-design the entire operation.

Of course, this wasn't possible and we were left placing our trust in the mediation process and our skills.

Second: the interviews that had generated this list of problems were followed immediately by a series of bilateral mini-mediations. These were planned to break some of the interpersonal impasses that stood in the way of any progress at the group level.

Each mini-mediation relied on the consensus approach, now applied at the micro level. Various pairs of key players worked through issues that troubled their relationships and the degree of trust they felt toward one another. Lowered levels of trust in each other had in turn influenced the relative commitments individuals were prepared to make to the company. Indeed, lowered trust in one another influenced the directors' concepts of the firm, their entire orientation to it, from organization and structure to share equity and provisions for distribution of profits.

Third: after this series of successful mini-mediations, where some individuals appeared on several occasions to work out problems they had with others, a large group session was planned. A confidential letter was sent to each key player, wherein the positive steps that had taken place thus far were outlined, and wherein I emphasized the fact that there were both discrete disputes and underlying conflicts facing them. I recommended we proceed as follows:

1. We work all day, with lunch provided;
2. We proceed with a mediation format:
   (a) ground rules will be clarified (i.e., the session is "without prejudice")
   (b) each participant will give a brief (10 minute) opening statement which will include the dispute(s) he wishes to deal with and a preliminary outline of personal objectives with respect to the dispute and future involvement in Bacma
   (c) the order of issues to be addressed will be decided by consensus
   (d) bilateral sessions and private caucuses will take place as necessary.

The fist mediation session with five directors resulted in significant progress on two thorny issues that had aggravated them, responsibility for a law suit against the company and an agreement to repay a large amount of unrecovered drawings by one of the directors. The areas remaining to be addressed were mapped out and a commitment to work at resolution of all differences was given.

Fourth: the second session, lasting a full day, also proceeded as a mediation. With the two obstacles removed in the first meeting everyone was able to turn their attention to larger, corporate level issues. A visioning exercise emerged naturally and various views of the future of the company were explored, and models of operation. This led to redefinition of the company from a profit-centred model to a corporate model. From that model, details with respect to executive management, personnel, and distribution of profit and loss were hammered out.

Bacma International is just one of many success stories that demonstrate the power of consensus processes.

The entire intervention was completed within a one month period at a fraction of the costs of conventional services. Most importantly, the company and its people were rejuvenated and reports are that the firm is healthy, profitable and expanding through acquisitions.

Consensus processes have proven themselves in the business world, where mediation has been used successfully in a range of commercial disputes. They are also suited to complex multi-party disputes that are typically found in government.

One of the strongest examples is the Helpline Reconciliation Model Agreement.

The Helpline Reconciliation Model Agreement

The consensus process was used to negotiate an unprecedented agreement between victims of child abuse and the institutions in Ontario responsible for their care.

This consensus process has come to be known as the Helpline Reconciliation Model Agreement. The Agreement was arrived at through mediation and an inter-related set of consensus building activities that took over two years to complete.

The participants in the Agreement were: Helpline, an association of some 400 former students of St. Joseph's Training School for Boys, Alfred, and St. John's Training School for Boys, Uxbridge; the Brothers of the Christian Schools of Ottawa; the Government of Ontario; the Archdiocese of Ottawa; and the Archdiocese of Toronto.

The Agreement sought a human healing process between men who reported sexual and physical abuse at the two schools, and the government and religious institutions involved. It attempted to achieve the objectives of social justice, reconciliation, and restoration of harm done. The Agreement was entitled the Helpline Reconciliation "Model" Agreement, in part because it includes the design of a participant-managed model for redressing the victims; and in part because the Agreement is a model, an unprecedented use of consensus processes in the public sector.

The $16 Million Agreement includes the following provisions:

‣ apologies by those responsible where injuries are found to have occurred
‣ claims by former students will be submitted for review to a Reconciliation Process Implementation Committee. The Committee will forward the claims to members of the Criminal Injuries Compensation Board of Ontario, who will receive evidence and information from the claimants and determine entitlement to payment for pain and suffering
‣ the Agreement contains a formula by which the Christian Brothers will increase the award of the CICB
‣ an Opportunity Fund has been created to provide validated claimants medical/dental services, vocational rehabilitation, educational upgrading and literacy training
‣ as a gesture of good faith, a contribution will be made toward wages which were lost for work done by the students and for which they were not paid
‣ counselling services for Helpline members are provided
‣ a Recorder will publish the experiences of former students who wish to be heard and make recommendations to prevent abuse in institutional settings
‣ the participants, other than Helpline, are paying the costs of implementing the Agreement and are also paying Helpline's operational and legal expenses

Background

The idea for exploring the potential of a mediated negotiation settlement in the Helpline case originated with Helpline, and their legal counsel, Mr. Roger Tucker.

In the summer of 1990, Mr. Tucker and his colleague, Ms. Evita Roche, queried the author as to whether mediation might be used in such a case, especially as the victims were seeking a form of redress that the courts would not be able to deliver. The victims wanted an apology from the government and the church, counselling for emotional trauma in the aftermath of sexual and physical abuse, opportunities for rebuilding their lives, financial compensation for pain and suffering, and a form of public reporting that would tell the story and hopefully prevent abuse in the future.

The idea of a voluntary "assisted negotiation" among all the parties, with a view to co-designing a mechanism that would meet the various needs of victims and would be based on the interests of all the parties was envisaged.

But how could this be done? How would Helpline be able to get the government and the church to the table? How many parties were there? Who would pay for the process? Who could mediate? Was mediation the right term in this case?

Convening

I knew that a "convenor" would be necessary to move the process from an idea and a hope, to a practical reality. The Convenor determines whether mediation is appropriate by:

‣ identifying the parties
‣ identifying the issues
‣ determining party willingness to participate in a consensus process
‣ determining acceptability of the mediator

The convenor had to be someone with the power of moral persuasion and the eminence to bring the parties to the table to participate in the process.

That convenor was Douglas Roche. Mr. Roche was former Canadian Ambassador to the UN on Disarmament, a prominent Catholic, and a man of immense commitment to his fellow human beings.

When Douglas Roche prepared for his first round of visits to several of the key parties, for the purpose of inviting them to participate in mediation, we considered a number of issues.

First, we wanted to be certain that all of the relevant parties were identified. While some were known to Helpline as being key parties, we were less certain of others. Were any parts of the Montreal-based Catholic Church involved? Where would insurance companies fit in? How many parties were likely to sit down to the table when everyone had been convened? Since the Government of Ontario was involved, how open would the process have to be?

I suggested several items be clarified from the outset, and that these might become "ground rules". The process would be voluntary, each party would have a veto over the process and the person of the mediator; the process would be without prejudice, anything said at the meeting would not be used by the parties if litigation was pursued later on; the process would be non-binding, in that anyone could walk away and the final agreement would only be binding if those who are party to it agreed to be bound by it.

We felt it would also be important to clarify that participation is not equal to an admission of guilt. Participating was a matter of moral responsibility, where the focus would be on the future, on healing and reconciliation rather than on the past, on culpability. Criminal charges had been laid against individual Brothers and they should go their own course, completely independent of this process which was at the institutional level.

Somehow, in language that Douglas believed each party would appreciate, we needed to communicate that the mediation was to design a process for redressing the harm done. The process would be designed collaboratively and it would have to satisfy each and every party who participated.

Mr. Roche's convening efforts elicited the following list of needs of the potential participants:

▸ a need for more information about the proposed conflict resolution process, about mediation, and about past successes with this approach
▸ a need for security, through assurances that culpability is not at issue, that the civil could be separated from the criminal so that defence of criminal charges would not be prejudiced in any way
▸ a need for certainty, in that participants wanted assurances that the members of Helpline were in fact fully represented by their spokesman, Mr. David McCann; that Mr. McCann had authority to negotiate
▸ a need for confidentiality
▸ a need to build trust

At the first meeting, attended by representatives of the Ontario Government, the Church and the Christian Brothers of Ottawa, I was introduced as an expert advisor.

The "maps" of mediation processes and principles of mediation, which I kept in mind as we moved forward, proved very helpful in providing a broad framework for proceeding (and for assessing "where we were"). I took quite literally the working definition of mediation as "assisted negotiation". My analysis of parties and problems relied heavily on negotiation theory as developed by Professor Roger Fisher and his colleagues at the Program on Negotiation at Harvard Law School. For guidance in clinical matters, I relied on the sensitivities I had developed in my group work with men who abuse women, including anger expression and group dynamics. For insights into the overall objective of the process—that is, reconciliation and healing—I looked to models of restorative justice, based on pioneering efforts in victim-offender reconciliation and the work on "social responsibility" ongoing at National Associations Active in Criminal Justice, Ottawa.

The "maps" of mediation which we followed included the 5-stage Model outlined in our discussion of Bacma International, and a macro view, the 3-stage Model. The 3-stage Model is often described as:

stage one   — pre-negotiation (or convening);
stage two   — "assisted negotiation" (or mediation);
stage three — implementation and follow-up.

Both models, and an understanding of interpersonal interaction, the type of questions to expect and to ask, and the technical dimensions of what should transpire in each stage were particularly helpful.

The subject of ground rules did get addressed at the first meeting. We outlined the three stages of a complex, multiparty multi-issue process. The seeds of a win-win outcome were sown, and the strategic dimensions of negotiating with the assistance of a mediator were explained. My objective here was not just to give them the map that was inside my head, but to have them seize upon one of the most important strategic dimensions of negotiation. Specifically, I wanted them to be familiar with the concept of their Best Alternative to A Negotiated Agreement (BATNA). I wanted each to weigh their alternatives to participating in this process and to have that alternative firmly placed in the back of their minds.

As outlined in our discussion of theory, my belief is that a negotiated agreement, arrived at with or without the assistance of a mediator, is only respectable if it is better than what any party could achieve away from the table. This sets a standard, or threshold above which the negotiated agreement must rise. This will encourage the production of "rich" agreements. The Helpline Process would have to yield a very rich agreement if it was going to meet the many and sometimes unique objectives of the parties.

As it turned out, Mr. Roche was the consummate Convenor. The meeting went extremely well and I personally had my first insight into the parties and my first conviction that this was doable. In addition to our own background analysis of the motivation for each participant to continue I was convinced that reconciliation and healing had much more than a strategic role to play in this process.

Assisted Negotiation

After several meetings the process was beginning to pick up speed. The momentum was accelerated in the fall of 1991 when Michael Cochrane, who was the Government's representative at the time, introduced an informal without prejudice proposal to meet the immediate needs of Helpline.

Helpline responded favourably to the proposal and with input from others it became the focus of the process for the next four months.

From a process point of view, I was pleased that the proposal had placed the issue of "quantification" of need on the table. The "parties" thus far had begun to develop a sense of who Helpline was and what its membership was composed of, but only by heresy and based on impressions of the Helpline negotiating team. But real insight into the allegations, a valid and trustworthy measure of victim need was not before them. Just how serious was the alleged abuse? How many victims were we talking about? Where and when did the abuse take place? What were the *members* of Helpline really looking for in the process?

In order to move forward, I sensed we had to slow down. Douglas Roche would have the difficult task of keeping the parties focused on the high road and support their efforts to maintain their own constituencies; I would support considerable informal dialogue among the parties while my company undertook the analysis of a major survey of the victims' needs.

An Analysis of St. Joseph's and St. John's Survivors of Child Abuse Survey and Assessment of Needs

Two social workers administered a 36-page questionnaire to 152 members of Helpline, and with funding support from the Ontario-based The Fund for Dispute Resolution, my company, Concorde Inc. analyzed the data.

What is especially important for our consideration is the way in which this information was jointly commissioned by the parties, the value of neutral assessment, and the critical role of a "protocol for management of the analysis".

The survey of victims, estimated as producing over 11,000 pages of raw data, was clearly a turning point in the process. The parties accepted my advice that the survey be analyzed by an impartial third party. If they were going to have confidence in the results I knew they must trust the analyst. For the first time, the process would get a thorough picture of the victims and their needs.

The questionnaire sought information with respect to:

▸ the school attended and the dates of entry and discharge;
▸ the abuse, including:
—assault;
—severe assault;
—sexual assault;
—severe sexual assault;
▸ the effects of the abuse on later life;
▸ employment, family and educational history;
▸ criminal record;
▸ employment upgrading needs;
▸ educational upgrading needs;
▸ literacy upgrading needs;
▸ wages lost while at training school;
▸ counselling needs;
▸ apologies;
▸ public examination and review;
▸ medical needs;
▸ dental needs;
▸ compensation and settlement information.

An Extended Negotiation Session

Despite the progress that was being made on meeting the immediate needs of the victims and the background work on the Survey and its analysis, the process continued to face pressures emanating from Helpline's need for movement. I assumed that Helpline's membership was putting pressure on its negotiating team. Clearly, individual Helpline members were having their own problems and stresses as they became witnesses in the criminal trials which were taking place independent of these discussions. This, along with the Survey, had forced many men to re-visit the trauma they had experienced years before in the training schools. This stressor alone was causing reverberations in the process and Helpline may have been increasing the intensity at the table to drive the process toward a settlement before its own membership disintegrated.

Helpline was pressing for a commitment to a deadline of June 30, 1992 and they pushed for an extended negotiation session in February.

The agenda would be full; it turned out that the session was pivotal. Planning on leaving the first evening open for a joint planning session on how the participants would like to tackle the largest item, the General Plan of Reconciliation, the session would cover the many agenda items, including Report of the Survey of Helpline members and the Survey Analysis; Report of the Insurance meeting of February 5; Implementation of the Interim Proposal (counselling, vocational training and education, medical/dental); Funding commitments; manner of securing institutional commitment to model; manner of implementing model. (Just in case that wasn't enough we also included "other"; and sure enough, there were other items that were brought forward).

The importance of this event, in addition to the progress on substantive items, was the spirit it built among the negotiators. There was time on the first evening and over meals to socialize together and build relationships. It was an opportunity for some healing and reconciliation to take place.

Drafting the Agreement: Use of the
Single Negotiated Text

By late April the parties were 8 weeks away from their self-imposed deadline of June 30, 1992. So much still remained unresolved and the sheer volume of information exchange, sub-group work, attention to internal matters within each party was such that reaching a final agreement seemed unrealistic at the current pace.

I recommended to Douglas that a critical path needed to be constructed to ensure that the process delivered on time. It had occurred to me that the parties needed to take more ownership for the process, including the design of the critical path itself.

40

Douglas agreed and when he introduced me at the next meeting, saying I would present a critical path to the group, I worried that he might be disappointed.

My thinking was that I could put a large chart in front of them, marking the 8 weeks to June 30, and give them the pieces of the puzzle that needed to be dealt with if they were to succeed.

An academic effort on my own to construct a critical path would have seen me making decisions about ideas and issues still "floating around". I didn't know which ones would find their way into a settlement or where they should be placed on the time line. Such decisions, I realized, needed to be made by the group. They would have to confirm which element would be addressed and in what order to bring closure for June 30.

So I somewhat awkwardly introduced my intervention as something like a parlour game. I had each of the elements I could think of marked on a small card in large print and I put them on the wall in a random order, surrounding the time line chart that showed 8 weeks from the present to June 30.

Some of the "things to do" were: negotiate a package (including pain and suffering, lost wages, medical/dental; provision for research on child abuse and its prevention; the role of a Fact Finder—terms of reference and selection of a candidate); develop a sunset provision; develop a process for validating individual claimants; keep each constituency informed as we go; agree on an implementation and monitoring mechanism.

This group exercise, although quite simplistic, was remarkably helpful. It demonstrated the amount of work necessary, it put the problem graphically before the whole group; it elicited constructive responses and collaboration in "placing" each item on the critical path.

Douglas Roche seized the moment. He invited volunteers to take on elements of the puzzle, and got strong responses from various individuals and groups on everything. He then asked me, that after a round of consultations which would follow the meeting, to draw up the document which would then become the "single negotiating text."

With input from everyone who had volunteered to work on specific topics, I prepared two drafts of the agreement, the second of which was a 17-section document ready for the June 8–9 meeting.

On June 2, 1992 I sent the following memorandum to all the participants in the process:

> As noted in the minutes (of the May meeting), participants will be working from a single negotiated text. A primary reason for proceeding based on a single negotiated text is that participants focus their attention on the text itself, in essence the "draft agreement". The procedure for developing this type of text is that the participants "negotiate" the text during meetings. Revisions to the text will incorporate changes which are the result of consensus, and will reflect an increasingly narrower range of alternatives on particular items when agreement has not yet been reached. Participants are encouraged to give me exact proposed language on items and even their marked-up copies of the text in hand and in each successive draft I will attempt to reflect the emerging consensus.

The single negotiated text was revised over and over again. At one point it was revised editorially by Peter Lauwers, lawyer for the Archdiocese of Toronto, for the purposes of putting it into legalese. By the time the marathon negotiation session was upon us, in late June, the parties were working on Draft 5. That text was revised several times, and some parts of it were re-worked many times before the final text was approved for ratification.

Marathon Negotiation Session
Twenty-nine hours of intense negotiations were not enough to produce a final text that all could agree to. Despite untiring efforts, we were confronting hours, even days more of fine-tuning that would be required before the Agreement would be acceptable for signature by all parties.

Nevertheless, I contend that critical momentum toward resolution came early in the session with Bishop O'Brien's sympathetic response to Helpline's request for apologies and, in particular, with the willingness of Tom Marshall, the negotiator for the Government, to meet Helpline's request for apologies. I also contend that a crucial moment was arrived at in that marathon session when an agreement, for all intents and purposes, was reached. It was a moment that I could witness, perhaps, because I had the luxury of being detached.

42

It came with a personal validation of the victims when the principle of individual choice was agreed to by Mr. John Nelligan, the negotiator for the Christian Brothers of Ottawa.

Implementation and Follow-up

When negotiating the Helpline Reconciliation Model Agreement the parties constructed a mechanism for implementing the agreement, and for resolving any disputes which might arise during implementation. This is the task of the Reconciliation Process Implementation Committee.

The Committee is comprised of representatives of each party to the Agreement, and it is chaired by Mr. Roche.

The Committee is responsible for processing the applications of any former student of the two training schools who wishes to appear before a specially constituted panel of the Ontario Criminal Injuries Compensation Board (CICB).

Testing the Agreement for Win-Win Competitiveness

The Agreement was negotiated using the consensus approach. It represents an unprecedented effort of this nature and it will be tested by reality and scholars in years to come.

In a press conference in August, 1992, the Agreement was described as representing "choices made by Helpline and other participants from among available options, and in the best interest of assisting Helpline's membership."

The question remains: was the Agreement a good outcome?

Our own post-mortem, conducted several months after the Agreement was ratified, led to the following conclusions.

First, the rights of the parties appear not to be compromised. All parties had legal representation throughout the process.

Second, we can see the Agreement from a new perspective by stepping back from micro issues and place the process and Agreement in the broader context of Conflict Resolution. Based on our analysis, the Helpline Reconciliation Model Agreement opens up new avenues for individual choice and fulfilment of individual needs. As individual victims move through the process, experience empowerment, and as the parties are placed in circumstances, such as giving and receiving apologies, discussing and meeting individual needs, opportunities for healing and a realization of their "vision to reconcile" will occur.

Finally, we can test the process and the Agreement against the best alternative available to the parties, that is, against litigation or some other adversarial form of disputing. Is the Agreement better than that which litigation might have produced? How does win-win apply here? If it does apply, how is competitiveness enhanced?

A "Good" Outcome?

Our assessment is that the Agreement is a "rich" agreement and one that meets the fourfold generic tests popularly applied to outcomes in the conflict resolution field. That is, the Agreement seems to be *fair*, *wise*, *efficient* and, consequently, we can assume it will *endure*.

It is hard to imagine how litigation would have yielded such a settlement.

If we were to ask whether all parties perceive the Agreement as *fair*, given that they each had a hand in crafting it and were not obliged to ratify it, it is reasonable to assume that each, in their own way and likely for very different reasons, would say it was fair.

Was it *wise*? Again, the inclusion in the Agreement of such features as the appointment of a Recorder whose purpose includes making recommendations designed to prevent any future abuse in institutional settings, and the provisions to equip victims to carry on more effectively with their lives all reinforce the sense that the negotiators looked beyond the immediate, and deeper than the instrumental, to develop a wise agreement. Future considerations, ongoing relationships, prevention of recurrence of abuse, and contingencies which may arise during the implementation period were anticipated. Mechanisms to address them were included in the Agreement.

On the question of *efficiency*, we must assess whether the transaction costs of negotiating the Agreement were reasonable, even economical; and whether the Agreement itself reflects a maximizing of joint gain. Was this a win-win outcome? That is, did the parties who negotiated the agreement leave as little value on the table as possible. Were they able to extract as much as possible from the potential each and all brought to the table?

The transaction costs have not been disclosed but anecdotal reports of those involved indicate that they are considerably less than they would have been if the dispute was litigated; and the cost of a public inquiry, the constructive dimensions of which are provided for in this Agreement by creating the position of the Recorder, would have been on the order of ten or more times the cost of the Recorder.

In addition to this "transaction cost" test of efficiency, the variety and creativity of the elements of the Agreement all suggest the Agreement meets the second efficiency criterion—maximizing joint gain.

The richness of the Agreement is found in features such as a non-adversarial system for validating a victim/claimant while protecting the interests of the institutions against abuse; a participant-operated Reconciliation Process Implementation Committee; provisions for counselling to victims and their families; and opportunity to apply for compensation for wages that were lost when the students were enroled in the training schools but worked without pay on neighbouring farms.

A fair, wise, and efficient agreement will likely *endure*. Failure to honour commitments or other problems which might result in impasses and breakdown are addressed through provisions for resolving any dispute which may arise during implementation.

It can be claimed that this Agreement passes the test of a "good" outcome. It is a win-win agreement. Lowered transaction costs, positive working relationships between the parties involved, and creative solutions to help put victims back to productive lives all enhance health, productivity, and arguably, our competitiveness. Furthermore, more effort, time and money might have been expended in other processes. Those resources are now available for other constructive uses.

I am satisfied that reconciliation and healing as it is made possible through the Agreement would not have come from litigation or adversarial processes, that transaction (legal and process) costs would have been much higher; and that, if anything, the vision to reconcile and restore those people in Canadian society who were touched by abuse in the two institutions was facilitated by the consensus process used here.

The Helpline Reconciliation Model Agreement is an example of how governments can apply Win-Win Competitiveness.

CHAPTER EIGHT

Skills, Tools and Systems for Success

THE consensus approach is the way of the future.
There are three essential elements that must be developed in any effort to build our Win-Win Competitiveness. People must be given:

‣ the *skills* of conflict resolution,
‣ the *tools* for conflict analysis, and
‣ the *systems* of conflict prevention (policy, procedures and mechanisms to support the application of the tools and the skills).

These elements are needed whether you are thinking of applications on the job at the most direct level, such as improving the way people get along together; or whether you are a government regulatory agency looking for better ways to get private industry to comply with regulations.

Education, skills development, and practice in the use of new techniques of problem solving and dispute resolution have to be provided, and new tools of analysis of problems must be tested, refined, and modified to meet the challenges, regardless of where you choose to apply Win-Win Competitiveness.

Comparative advantage now hinges, not just a country's natural resources, its access to labour, or its proximity to markets, but on its technological prowess—on the sophistication of its infrastructure, in the efficiency of suppliers and, most importantly, on the education and skill levels of its workforce.[10]

Win-Win Competitiveness as a new comparative advantage can be built—not in Japan, not in Germany, not the U.S.A.—but right here in Canada.

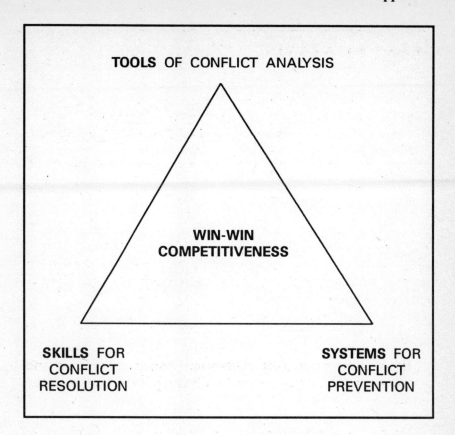

Re-Tooling for Win-Win Competitiveness

CHAPTER NINE

Persuasive Scenarios for Adopting Consensus Processes in Business

*" What happened and what **could happen** "*

Consider CalTech

CalTech was first incorporated by three friends to advance their interest in AIDS treatment research. Three years ago, the three principals of CalTech were Dr. Matthew White, Mr. Barry Stuart, and Mr. Ralph Majors. White is a biochemist trained at McGill, who has spent the last ten years of his career conducting research in pursuit of an antigen which will treat AIDS; Stuart is a wealthy businessman whose first money was inherited but has since been put to good use and has yielded high return; and Majors is the Dean of a business college in eastern Ontario.

The three friends have known each other since under-graduate studies at Queen's University. They are now in their early fifties, and their families have all grown up together, visiting and vacationing together over the years. Their wives are now shareholders in CalTech, along with two lawyers and some other closer friends. Altogether, there are seven share-holders, although Stuart has invested the most capital.

When Dr. White presented the idea that CalTech be formed, he proposed that Stuart be Chairman, and largest investor; and that Majors be CEO. Each would thus contribute on a somewhat equal basis to the new company, giving what they most easily could. Both Majors and Stuart agreed to the idea, believing in the value of an AIDS treatment R & D company; they felt White was close to a breakthrough after years of hard work, and they knew the cause was well worth their effort. Financial success at the end of the day would be gravy on top of the sense of personal achievement in their joint contribution to humanity.

Two years of business flew by. White was busy in the lab—literally using a number of research facilities provided through the generosity of medical colleagues—and the only business issues were those of making investments for equipment and materials, expanding the circle of shareholders, and seeing to it that the books were in order.

Some tension, however, had arisen among the business friends. Majors found that White never kept him posted on developments but would drop requests on the others, expecting immediate action. Dr. White also pressed Majors to apply for foundation funding but gave no real support in the application processes. Stuart recognized that his old friend, Matt White, was an eccentric genius and he continued to believe in him; although he felt the tension between White and Majors. Stuart also thought Majors lacked the people management skills to handle White, although he was very impressed with Majors' business acumen.

One year ago, everything at CalTech began to accelerate. Dr. White reported that he was going to move to a clinical trial stage in his research and that he had received an invitation to work in a major university research hospital. An old friend of White's was able to make the lab available; he would see to it that White had full access to the hospital's research facilities and resources. The hospital's research committee had reviewed White's work, and published papers, and believed he was on to something big.

Dr. White had called the meeting of CalTech and made the exciting announcement. During his presentation, White also mentioned that some money, maybe $50,000, would be needed up front and that the hospital would want to take out a patent on anything White produced.

Majors blew up. He could not believe that White would pursue anything of the sort. Here the three of them had been ploughing everything they each could give into the company, and White was about to give it all away!

Majors looked to Stuart for support. Stuart, typically non-assertive in Majors' view, asked whether his investment would be paid back. White said he wasn't sure.

White declared how he had finally found support from the medical establishment for his life's work—and he insisted that he had no choice but to take advantage of a window of opportunity that would close quickly. He was not the only researcher looking for facilities and support like this.

Stuart re-offered that his primary objective had been to see White's work come to life—profits, while important, were secondary. Majors felt betrayed and alienated. He had attended all the meetings, he had written several proposals to granting foundations and presented them at meetings across the country, he had kept the business matters in order and had not been paid for many of his services.

Majors blew up at White and White responded sharply that Majors was just a pedestrian, money-hungry WASP, driven by a money-hungry Chink, referring to Majors' Chinese wife, who White had never really liked.

The meeting broke up bitterly.

Within days, Majors filed a letter of suit against White.

White called Stuart looking for help.

Stuart didn't know what to do. It looked like CalTech, his money, and his friendships were lost.

In fact, everything stalled as the lawyers for each side took over, each partner now represented in a legal battle.

That's what happened at Caltech.

Here's what could have happened:

‣ The Shareholders Agreement could have had a dispute resolution clause in it. Such a clause would have allowed each and any of the partners to initiate a non-adversarial process to deal quickly and cost-effectively with this dispute and impasse.

‣ A sample clause is: It is agreed that the parties to this dispute will use mediation, and then arbitration as alternatives to litigation in the event of any dispute arising under this agreement.

‣ It is probable that Mr. Stuart could have used the clause and an independent mediator could have set about working through the personal and business problems confronted by the three old friends.

‣ CalTech could be put back on the tracks within weeks rather than months, or even years, when time is of the essence in this young company's life.

Consider Hurst's

Hurst's Ladies Wear had no idea how good an employee they got when Sara West was hired. Two years ago, Sara, who had stayed home to raise her kids to school age, and who at one time owned and operated her own craft shop, decided it was time to re-enter the workforce. She was thirty-six years old, experienced in retail, and her personal obligations were such that she could be a flexible employee, able to work irregular part-time hours.

The Manager who interviewed Sara thought Sara was a personable, older woman and she gave Sara a job immediately. For the first year, Sara worked with an unusual devotion to her job which was a retail sales clerk in one of Hurst's chain stores located in a mid-sized Canadian town. Then things began to sour.

The Manager, who liked Sara, found that Sara was beginning to get sticky about her hours; Sara also seemed less motivated, although her relations with customers were always good. And furthermore, Sara sold more product than anyone else in the store.

The Manager asked Sara what the problem was—and discovered that an employee who otherwise made little noise and got along so well with everyone, was very upset. Sara explained that the Assistant Manager, a woman in her mid-twenties, was systematically hassling Sara. Sara informed the manager that the other employees (four in the last year) had quit because of the Assistant Manager.

The Manager said she appreciated Sara's view, and acknowledged that Sara was probably right. The Assistant Manager was valuable to the store because of her bookkeeping abilities, although she lacked interpersonal skills. The Manager, a non-confrontational type of person, did nothing else.

Several months passed and the Regional Manager of Hurst's visited Sara's store. Sara hoped that the behaviour of the Assistant Manager would be the subject of discussion between Sara's store Manager and the Regional Manager. Sara was convinced that the Assistant Manager was insecure, incompetent as a supervisor, and was the reason so many other good clerks had left.

Hurst's had a reputation for a high turnover rate and seemed not to care. They also kept raising sales quotas, relied on part-time student help, and gave little to employees to make them feel happy about working. On top of this reputation, Sara was sure the local Assistant Manager made things worse.

Sara took the first opportunity to ask the store Manager about her meeting with the Regional Manager: "Had she raised the problem with the Assistant Manager?". The answer was "No". The store Manager acknowledged that Sara was probably right about the Assistant Manager but that everybody, including the Manager herself, had to learn to cope with her.

Six months later, Sara was almost totally de-motivated and the stress in attempting to put up with the Assistant Manager's harassment was serious enough that Sara was taking the problem home.

Sara's husband had told her to challenge the management system, or quit. He wasn't very sympathetic and while his suggestion probably made sense, it wasn't very easy to do. Sara didn't want to quit her job; she really liked sales, and was just building her self-confidence after being out of the job market for ten years. Furthermore, how could she confront management? She had already raised the issue twice with the Store Manager, who she also liked personally but found weak in this situation. Should she take the matter right to the Regional Manager? What to do?

Two more women joined and left Hurst's over the next four months. Sara now did her shift, and gave little more to the job. The Assistant Manager kept her distance now because Sara had snapped at her one day when the Assistant Manager had embarrassed Sara in front of a regular customer. But the Assistant Manager had the upper hand and did all she could to make it hard on Sara.

One day the Regional Manager dropped in unannounced while the Store Manager was off. Sara was on duty and when asked how it was going she blurted out her problem.

In fact, she began to cry as she told the Regional Manger about the past two years and the negative impact of the Assistant Manager on employees, and ultimately, on the profitability of the store. Sara was embarrassed she had been moved to tears.

The Regional Manager showed some signs of sympathy and noted that the Store Manager had said something at one time about supervisory relations within the store, without giving much detail. The Regional Manager told Sara that she had told the Store Manager that: "In a dispute between an employee and a supervisor, our policy is the supervisor is always right".

Sara could not believe her ears!

Within days she quit her job, worried that quitting would be a blight on her employment record when she went elsewhere to look for work.

That's what happened at Hurst's Ladies Wear.

Here's what could have happened:

‣ Hurst's, like any other business, is trying to make a profit. Prepared to use part-time employees to cover most shifts, supported by a small full-time staff, Hurst's is losing an untold amount in worker productivity, and probably, in repeat business. The conflict resolution skills, and in-store procedures to keep Hurst's employees working smoothly are lacking. Sara should have been able to raise her concerns directly with her Manager who would have the skills and tools to intervene constructively, rather than avoiding the issue.

‣ Some remedies include:

(a) skills training for the Assistant Manager so that she is no longer incompetent in interpersonal relations, and no longer threatened by older, competent staff;

(b) a "manager as mediator" training course could have been given to the Store Manager so that she is equipped to mediate disputes between employees;

(c) an "employee complaint and suggestion" procedure could be in place so that employees can raise matters without fear of recrimination. In the event that Sara's Manager could not deal with the issue, Sara could have taken advantage of a management-approved mechanism for raising issues with the Regional Manager; and

(d) a corporate policy could be established to examine disputes in an open way, providing assurance to all concerned that the objective is not to blame anyone but to remedy problems to encourage positive, productive working relationships.

55

Consider Ingram Multipro

Ingram Multipro is a Taiwanese business that has grown from a small light assembly firm to an international corporation. Seven years ago it began an aggressive acquisition and expansion plan, targeting Canada, Belgium, and Holland as safe countries in which to invest.

The private sector in Belgium and Holland have shown a strong response to Ingram's initiatives, with joint ventures established on top of a reliable base of contracts between Ingram and several communications companies in the two countries.

Canada has been much slower, although the Canadians who have done business with Ingram's Taiwanese executives have demonstrated strong appreciation for cultural differences, making it pleasant for Ingram to do business with them, and the Canadians have always delivered on their end of the deal.

One recent exception concerns a Canadian defence industry supplier which has an agreement to provide parts to Ingram for assembly in Taiwan. The agreement between Ingram and Sparta Micro, a wholly owned Canadian company, is quite complex. Sparta receives pre-assembled units in its Calgary factory from a California manufacturer, where there is some Canadian content—a requirement of Canadian government funding which is provided to Sparta to support it during its developmental phase.

Sparta then ships the units with Canadian value added to Taiwan. Ingram adds a Belgium-produced de-coding device, and returns the units to Calgary for final assembly. The last stage really involves the simple fitting of the units into a Canadian-made casing which is designed for installation in Canadian fighter jets.

The Canadian company informed Ingram several months ago that it has an opportunity to sell the final units to the US government, where demand is much greater. Ingram responded favourably. It wasn't until Ingram's Belgium connection learned about the potential deal between Sparta and the US government that things got difficult.

The Belgian company reminded Ingram that the technology for the central de-coding device was designed in the USA, by a Cambridge-based R & D company, ERLON. ERLON has an exclusive agreement with Belgium, which Ingram had known about but never told Sparta.

Sparta has now become quite hostile toward Ingram, having received notice from ERLON that ERLON retains the patent on the de-coder and wishes Sparta to work directly with them on any plans Sparta has for expansion into the US market. Sparta is suing Ingram because it fears ERLON will move unilaterally with the US Department of Defence, thereby cutting Sparta out. And Sparta is uncertain of Ingram's loyalties. Ingram may simply set up with ERLON.

Ingram does not like to settle disputes by litigation. In fact, it is offended by the Canadian company's behaviour and feels threatened that Sparta and ERLON will move independently, eliminating Ingram from a thrust into the USA. Ingram has thus put pressure onto its Belgium partner to take whatever steps necessary to deter ERLON from any action.

This stalemate has ground future developments to a halt, and troubled current arrangements. Tensions are rising and no cost-effective alternatives to a complex legal battle seem available.

That's what happened at Ingram Multipro.

Here's what could have happened:

‣ The technology proprietorship and transfer issues could have been addressed at the beginning of the relationship, and the issues of legal jurisdiction could have been clarified and resolved before any conflict arose.

‣ The Canadian government could have worked with Canadian business to establish an international commercial mediation and arbitration system in concert with the Taiwanese and American Governments, among others. The dispute resolution process could include a fact finding stage conducted by an independent body, the convening of several non-adversarial work sessions to sort out the issues, determining which, if any, require mediation, arbitration, or the involvement of the courts.

LESSONS FROM THE THREE SCENARIOS

MODE (Essential Element)	APPLICATION	
	INTERNAL (within the organization)	**EXTERNAL** (with clients, competitors, suppliers, and special interest groups)
CONFLICT ANALYSIS TOOLS	‣ individual and group conflict management assessment instruments ‣ social climate tests, evaluation tools ‣ conflict theory and analysis ‣ problem-solving tools ‣ decision-making tools	‣ case selection or conflict analysis tools ‣ negotiation strategy frameworks and guidelines ‣ issues of contract, guidelines, implementation and enforceability
CONFLICT RESOLU-TION SKILLS	‣ negotiation ‣ peer mediation techniques ‣ group facilitation and team building skills ‣ neutral evaluation and assessment skills ‣ arbitration techniques ‣ consensus-building skills	‣ negotiation skills ‣ conflict resolution skills
CONFLICT PREVEN-TION SYSTEMS	‣ policies, procedures and mechanisms for internal dispute resolution ‣ corporate ombudsman ‣ preventative mediation program	‣ customer complaints and dispute resolution services ‣ participating in mediation and arbitration as an alternative to litigation ‣ association-level activities to prevent and resolve industry disputes

CHAPTER TEN

Re-Tooling for Win-Win Competitiveness in Your Workplace

IT is estimated that up to 30% of most supervisor's time is spent dealing with conflict on the job. Some managers will insist the level is more like 80%!

Unresolved conflicts must be managed constructively to avoid the cost to people directly and indirectly involved, and to the business itself.

Assuming that one of the central challenges of life is finding solutions to problems, it can be shown that our Western adversarial approach has failed in a number of critical areas.

The costs in personal and organizational energy and effectiveness, the downward pressure on our individual and organizational productivity, and the negative impact on our quality of life which results from the purely adversarial approach is obvious.

The fundamental division in the structure of most commercial and business enterprises in a capitalist economy is perhaps one of the most obvious and common cases that shows just how badly an adversarial approach can be. The adversarial approach in labour relations entails a litany of costs, from the need of employees to organize themselves to advance and protect their self-interest through collective bargaining laws and practices; reliance on the "strike" and the "lock out" as coercive tools to manage conflicts; grievance procedures that are formal, cumbersome and must be "arbitrated" by a judge whose job it is to impose a win-lose settlement on management and labour; and fundamental alienation in the workplace in the process of conceptualizing, producing, marketing and delivering products and services.

Worker stress, unresolved conflict on the job, industrial sabotage, and violence in the workplace are all now recognized as forms of conflict that are seriously impairing individual and organizational productivity, and hence, competitiveness.

The Canadian Mental Health Association reports that 10 to 15 per cent of the workforce is incapacitated by acute or chronic personal problems; this affects job performance. Studies show that troubled employees have three times as many accidents, four times the rate of absenteeism, make more health insurance claims; and are more likely to make mistakes at work.[11]

A 1991 survey by the Canadian Institute of Stress found that the typical employer thinks more than 25% of all sick time is rooted in employee stress; and as much as 70% of complaints being processed by Employee Assistance Programs relate to conflict on the job. Not in the home, but on the job.[12]

Judy Darcy, President, Canadian Union of Public Employees asserted in September 1992 that workplace violence should be considered an occupational hazard, a well-kept secret that most employers still chose to ignore."[13]

Representatives of management, representatives of labour, industrial health and safety workers, employee relations counsellors and productivity and quality control experts all recognize these facts. Some businesses are taking steps to bridge the gap that the adversarial approach creates and reinforces at all levels of the organization. Others are entrenching themselves in more extreme forms of adversarial behaviour, unable to imagine or practice a better way.

Time, money, individual and organizational energy and health, and internal employee and external business relations are all at risk in settings that use ineffective systems and procedures for the tasks of wealth creation and production, and for dispute resolution.

Efforts to Improve Canadian Worker Productivity

In the 1960s and 1970s, organizations sought to improve productivity by providing performance incentives to top managers who managed the most productive workers. In the 1980s an emphasis on good employer-employee relations as a factor in high productivity led naturally to the idea that participatory management could be a more effective way to motivate all employees. This approach has evolved in the 1990s into one that assumes high motivation is based on both participatory management *and* hard incentives to individual workers.

Despite the progressive aspects of this evolution, *conflict itself is now one of the greatest challenges facing management in an era of constraint*. Delayering and downsizing, concession bargaining practices, and uncertainty about job security have placed a premium on negotiation and conflict resolution skills in the workplace.

In addition to these employee relations strains, business people and businesses absorb a significant amount of other conflict at considerable costs. Examples include shoplifting that is either undetected or left unenforced if detected; bad debt when even those clients who appeared most trustworthy simply refuse or are unable to pay their bill; failure on the part of suppliers or service people to honour commitments so that products are not delivered, or they are faulty on receipt; unfulfilled service agreements and warranties on equipment; partner and shareholder hassles that lead to reduced contributions to the firm or result in unfair distribution of dividends or benefits; and in some cases various forms of corporate theft, including theft of product or service ideas, contracts that get redirected to competitors, patent and trade mark violations, and embezzlement.

Conflict: Now What?

The first thing most business people do if they are going to take any action in a conflict, maybe having unsuccessfully confronted the person they believe is responsible, is call their lawyer. Lawyers are trained to fight, to advocate on behalf of their clients in a adversarial legal system that rewards the skills of argument, debate, and the fine use of power within the law. But this system has failed. It costs too much. It takes too long. It destroys business relations. It produces one winner, one loser. It does not deliver creative solutions to business disputes.

Businesses are beginning to look for alternatives.

But any business wishing to adopt win-win approaches to enhance the firm's competitiveness will have to ensure that the essentials are in place before there can be a reasonable expectation of return on the investment. This will take time, money, and patience. Internal corporate capacity for win-win approaches must be complimented by external applications as well. A transformation of the corporate culture, new forms of leadership and re-organization will be required.

Serious questions are likely to surface: these questions, and resistance, will come from labour, *and* from management. Senior managers will ask:

"How much is this win-win business going to cost us, at the end of the day? What happened to the old idea that 51 beats 49 every time?"

Labour leadership may fear an erosion of its role if employees are truly empowered. They may no longer need representatives if they have direct input. They may no longer need to be organized along adversarial lines.

Sometimes, the aversion to taking a different approach to problems or to resolve a dispute is nothing more than a *personal* aversion to conflict on the part of the CEO. Delay, muddling through, or looking for help to overpower any opposition may appear to be the path of least resistance, or at least, of most personal comfort.

Most organizations that are contemplating consensus decision-making come to the idea through the "conflict resolution" door. They usually have experience with negotiation and encounter mediation in its more simple forms—perhaps in a family divorce matter or in collective bargaining situations when a mediator is appointed; soon they develop a richer sense of the potential applications of these tools. Thus, skill development to support individuals who are wishing to use win-win approaches is normally the first response in implementing win-win approaches. This level of preparedness (skills acquisition) is a necessary but insufficient "first wave". It falls short of the commitment required to ensure success.

Re-tooling for Success

The introduction of win-win approaches to the workplace is perhaps one of the most risky management innovations in recent times. Forms of win-win approaches such as employee empowerment, participatory management, teambuilding and various employee ownership programs turn explicitly on the sharing of power. They are a direct appeal to the creative faculties of all employees and they imply that there will need to be a change in the culture and communication style of most workplaces. They call for a new form of commitment with respect to resource allocation, role definition, and organizational follow-through.

A serious commitment to win-win approaches in the workplace will have great implications for needed change in atti-

SOURCES OF CONFLICT FOR COMPANIES

SOURCES WITHIN THE COMPANY	Interpersonal	‣ stresses arising from office or home ‣ office gossip
	Hierarchies	‣ labour/management ‣ supervisor/employee ‣ seniority
	Duties	‣ risk taking: personal initiative versus "playing it by the rules" ‣ responsibility and accountability ‣ different duties
	Perceived Inequities	‣ ethnic, racial tensions ‣ sexual harassment ‣ full-time versus employees on contract
	Social Political Economic Trends	‣ affirmative action and pay equity ‣ technological change ‣ downsizing ‣ aging workforce

SOURCES OUTSIDE THE COMPANY	Your Market	‣ service, liaison, support to clients ‣ suppliers
	Economic Pressures	‣ interest rates and financing ‣ recession ‣ competition from domestic and foreign companies ‣ changing markets
	Political Pressure	‣ government regulations ‣ trade agreements ‣ special interest groups
	Environment	‣ air, water, noise pollution ‣ natural resources ‣ waste management

EFFECTS OF UNRESOLVED CONFLICT ON COMPANIES

INTERNAL	EXTERNAL
‣ Energy is directed away from work ‣ Negative effect on motivation ‣ Erodes team effort and team-building ‣ Exacerbates differences between people ‣ Costs money	‣ Affects the perception of the company in the community ‣ Disrupts business relationships ‣ Costs money

tudes and in skills development. The process of policy development will change as an emphasis will be placed on negotiation rather than consultation; management practice of DAD (decide, announce and defend) will be out; and operational procedures will need to support a more flexible assignment and execution of tasks.

Otto Brodtrick's work, conducted in the context of the Auditor General of Canada's Report in 1988, showed that well-performing public sector organizations feature an emphasis on people, participative leadership, innovative work styles, and strong client orientation. These characteristics imply a certain amount of attention to win-win approaches, underlining what can be accomplished when such approaches are put into action.[14]

In the private sector, similar observations apply. Experiments with team building, new forms of leadership, and participatory management schemes, while requiring considerable adjustment in most cases, are proving to be advantageous with respect to productivity and competitiveness.[15]

A disciplined, sustained effort, and the willingness to encounter failure and to make changes based on experience will be necessary to implement win-win approaches. Failure to pursue the course of action with integrity could lead to a very serious reactionary period. Raising expectations among employees and failing to follow through with a commitment to meet them is likely worse in most cases than leaving things as they were.

Experience to-date shows that both public sector and private organizations are expressing a need for assistance with "employee empowerment" and "team building" but most are willing to go only so far. There is a tendency to enlist employees and outside Organizational Development or Total Quality Management consultants in training sessions and intermittent interventions, but there is insufficient sustained effort to make the transition to a fully operationalized participatory workplace.[16]

Teams are formed around specific projects and given considerable latitude, but a complete transformation is not supported. For example, "directors" are not reclassified as "coordinators" when that is called for; front line staff, especially support staff, are not consulted as frequently as they were in the early stages of implementing the "new approach"; senior personnel fall back into old habits, including the practice of decide, announce and defend; and new policies and procedures necessary to support the changes are not initiated.

Furthermore, recent pressures to have "lean, mean machines" force a renewed myopia on the organization when, in fact, reality is placing a premium on a "global" "holistic" view that incorporates a fine sensitivity to change; a sensitivity that is developed through a scanning of the broad environment and a filtering of critical information which will impact the bottom line by inspiring innovation and streamlined production.

My experience and my company's approach to team building, employee empowerment, and participatory management is based primarily on our approach to consensus-building; we began with an identification of some of the obstacles to progress in these areas.

Obstacles to Team-building, Empowerment Participatory Management

‣ inappropriate concepts, such as work, power, and responsibility;
‣ inappropriate organization;
‣ poor communication;
‣ inappropriate work allocation;
‣ unsupportive corporate culture; and
‣ poor conflict management.

The following elements—purpose, leadership, culture, communication and commitment—can be used as a framework to measure the present environment and to guide the implementation of change in the direction of win-win approaches.

Purpose

This is the purpose of each team in a teambuilding exercise and the purpose (or mission statement) of the organization as a whole. Generally, efforts need to be directed by all employees toward the articulation of a clear and simple purpose. This mission exercise should ask, at the group level: what is our service, who is our client, how do we relate to the organization as a whole; and how do we monitor and evaluate our purpose. At the individual level, employees need to ask themselves: what is my role; who is my team; how do I relate to the team and how do I monitor and evaluate my performance.

65

The purpose should be collectively owned, modelled in behaviours internal to the organization; and externally, in the presentation of the organization to its clients and other organizations.

The purpose needs to be reviewed and modified, assessing it as to its validity as a response to the needs of both the clients and the members of the organization.

Leadership

Leadership should personify the vision. Leadership should model and support risk-taking. Leaders should be skilled in facilitating good decision-making as well as in making good decisions. The legitimacy of the authority of leaders is derived from those over whom the authority is exercised. Thus, decisions can be made and executed quickly when necessary. Consensus decision-making does not mean that everything bogs down.

Leaders should be seen as tough on problems, not on the people—they should "go to bat" for the team. Leaders in win-win organizations are visible, active, available—they are problem solvers. They are responsible for the timely management of the organization's workload, the coordination and assignment of tasks, and the allocation of resources. Some of their requisite skills include negotiation, consensus building, and mediation, apart from their technical expertise.

Culture

The culture of a workplace operating on win-win approaches is open, innovative, and responsive to change. It encourages practices such as "inventing before deciding", and guards at the same time against "group think".

Despite the fact that the culture recognizes and supports change it has an underlying characteristic of being consistent; it is reliable and supportive.

Humour is encouraged in the workplace, healthy environments are supported through employee assistance programs and conflict management mechanisms specifically customized for the setting.

Attention is paid to methods of measuring success and reacting to failure (taking into account the need for risk taking behaviour).

Communication

Personal contact, including face-to-face reinforcement of people by people is emphasized above electronic and formal communication. People interact in ways that show they are considerate of the needs and interests of others; this means communicating to others in the manner in which the other is most likely to be receptive. Anger and conflict are recognized as legitimate features of human interaction and people

---

TYPICAL ISSUES ADDRESSED IN EACH FACTOR AREA

PURPOSE
- [ ] at the organizational level, employees are asked: what is our service; who is our client; how does our unit relate to the organization as a whole; how do we monitor and evaluate our purpose
- [ ] at the individual level, employees are asked: what is my role; who is my team or unit; how do I relate to that unit; how is my performance monitored and evaluated

LEADERSHIP
- [ ] are leaders (supervisors) visible, active, available
- [ ] are leaders problem solvers
- [ ] are leaders seen as "going to bat" for employees
- [ ] do leaders organize the workload effectively and allocate tasks well

CORPORATE CULTURE
- [ ] is the corporate culture reliable and supportive
- [ ] is risk taking encouraged, such as making suggestions for change, taking initiative
- [ ] are programs such as Employee Assistance, a suggestion and complaint process, and dispute resolution mechanisms available

COMMUNICATION
- [ ] is there personal contact between supervisors and line employees
- [ ] is feedback, both negative and positive, given on a face-to-face basis, and frequently
- [ ] are methods such as employee newsletters or bulletins used to keep employees informed and in touch with each other
- [ ] are operating procedures and reporting requirements clear and effective— are staff and supervisors skilled in interpersonal communication, including conflict resolution and problem-solving techniques

Purpose + Leadership + Corporate Culture + Communication = Commitment

COMMITMENT
- [ ] are resource levels adequate
- [ ] do employees take responsibility
- [ ] is authority exercised legitimately and constructively
- [ ] are commitments that are made honoured

---

are skilled to express their anger constructively. People are taught to negotiate effectively and the role and importance of third party assistance is recognized from the outset: managers or designated peers function as mediators when necessary.

Commitment

Purpose + Leadership + Culture + Communication = Commitment

Commitment is achieved through the process of "building up—buying in". Resource levels and their allocation are adequate so that individuals and groups can be responsible. They have "response-ability". When resources aren't adequate, leadership is hard at work facilitating innovation internally and seeking additional resources externally.

Commitments that are made are honoured.

CHAPTER ELEVEN

Rebuilding our Communities Through Consensus Processes

The Context

1. More "Open" Conflict in Canada
2. Failure in the Courts
3. Make Way!—"Power to the People" is more than a slogan

More "Open" Conflict in Canada

Race riots, labour strikes and management lockouts that become volatile and infect the broader community, violence in schools, protracted disputes over proposed land uses or urban development schemes, and unresolved neighbourhood disputes over issues as apparently simple as where a fence belongs show the ineffectiveness of our conventional adversarial system of dispute settlement.

Most school authorities still rely on a punitive rather than a problem solving and collaborative approach to problems— things have become so bad in some schools that teachers are actually serving more as police than educators; community disputes that can't be nipped in the bud escalate so that force is necessary.

In all cases, low-level conflict, marked by frustration, poor communication, anger and bitterness can evolve to petty infractions and escalate to aggravated assaults, or in the case of group behaviour, to riots. At some point on the conflict continuum, conflict can take on the form of criminal behaviour.

Whether you are a victim of a break-and-enter crime or involved in a domestic dispute that escalates to violence and possibly even homicide, most crime grows out of conflict. Crime is conflict that involves the doing of harm, a violation of some sort that is deemed unacceptable in our society. Certain conflict behaviour is codified as crime.

We have traditionally worked to prevent crime mostly through deterrence and the threat of punishment, and by attempting to correct the offender after a specific crime has occurred. In either case, that is in our efforts to prevent crime or in dealing with offenders, statistics suggest we are not doing very well. Crime is on the increase in Canada, and our success in correcting or rehabilitating offenders has not really improved in the past two decades. In fact, we incarcerate more offenders per capita and we have more police per capita than most other "free" and "democratic" societies.

Crime is conflict and everywhere in Canada, at all levels —from interpersonal to inter-group—conflict abounds. To prevent crime, and to improve the quality of our communities we must learn more about conflict and how to manage it in our daily lives.

Even in routine business at City Hall, we are discovering the limits of adversarial approaches. For example, land development proposals and re-zoning applications now tend to turn into disputes. A citizen's group will contest the proposal; a government department will want to enforce environmental protection regulations, placing pressure on the developer.

The standard practice in these once routine matters is to place the case before a panel or quasi-judicial tribunal that treats the issues in an adversarial framework. Evidence is heard for each side's case, (and there may be many sides in complex, multi-issue disputes), experts for either side are called upon to show the strength of one position over another, the process is legalistic, involves formalized procedures, and at the end of the day—which is usually years after the dispute first arose—a decision is made by an "authority" who will effectively render one side a winner, the other a loser.

This process, of course, is often complemented by political lobbying and pressure tactics, generally resulting in even greater antipathy between the parties involved. Bad feelings and strained relationships are often the end product.

It is a fact that we are witnessing more open conflict in Canada than we have ever known. Unfortunately, despite our need for safety and peace, we are not coping with it very well.

Failure in the Courts

A scathing feature article in an 1992 issue of *Business Week* is entitled, "Guilty! Too many lawyers, too much litigation, too much waste. Business is starting to find a better way."[17] While the number of lawyers may or may not be a valid concern, it is clear that lengthy, procedure-ridden, and extremely costly adversarial approaches to disputes as practised in our justice system are failing us.

We Canadians are generally less litigious than our American neighbours, and Canadian business executives may not share the same critical view of the justice system as that set forth in the Business Week issue. But in Canada, commencing with the Askov case in Ontario, there has been an increasing discomfort with the way we do justice. Following Askov's case, the Ontario Courts dismissed many criminal cases simply because the courts were too backlogged. The rights of the accused to a speedy trial had been violated by the justice system itself.[18]

Discomfort with the justice system is perhaps felt the most and given its greatest expression by the very people who have the responsibility for managing it; they know first hand how overburdened the courts are, and how ineffective prison is, although they tend to ask for more of the same as a means of dealing with backlogs: more judges, more court administrators, more lawyers—and more prisons.

The backlogs may become so great in the next few years that alternative, non-adversarial forms of dispute resolution will be compelling for no other reason than their efficiency. But for individuals and businesspeople who must live with the excessively long delays before their case is even heard, and for the fifty percent of those that must come away losers —because that's the way the system is set up—the adversarial system has failed.

Mr. Justice R.E. Holland ruled on a dispute between *International Corona v. Lac Minerals* over the ownership of a $1 billion gold mine. When his decision was upheld on appeal, he commented that it would have taken only four days to settle the dispute if mediation techniques had been used. By going through the courts the case took over three years to come to trial—including weeks of pre-trial discovery—almost nine months of trial, and over two years of appeals in the Ontario Court of Appeal and the Supreme Court of Canada. It cost the parties involved millions of dollars in legal fees, and the taxpayer had to foot the bill for court rooms, court staff and judges.[19]

There will be cases that deserve to be treated in the courts. But these are few in number relative to the volume of disputes

71

in Canadian society, and in business. Lawyers will need to re-define their roles, develop new skills and serve clients differently in their efforts to achieve cost-effective dispute resolution. Without these changes, our lives and our businesses are placed on hold; our health and productivity suffer.

Make Way!—"Power to the People" is more than a slogan

In 1990, Oka, Kanasatake and Chateauguay became household words, the names of communities in Quebec where Indians were fighting with the government and where a police officer was killed. In 1992 we watched the first race riots in Toronto and a bitter strike by gold miners in Yellowknife has infected the whole community. The RCMP claim that nine miners who died underground during the strike were murdered. Management has called the incident an act of "industrial terrorism" and labour leaders claimed that management was out to break the union through the use of any tactic, including the employment of scab labour.

Also in 1992 Canadians overwhelmingly rejected the proposal to amend the constitution on the basis of the Charlottetown Accord, which had been unanimously endorsed by their political leaders from all parties.

What happened at Oka? Why did a dispute between Mohawk Indians and townsfolk over a proposed nine-hole addition to a golf course become a major conflict that mobilized Natives across Canada in sympathy of their Mohawk brothers and sisters? Why are we so suspicious of our political leaders?

What has happened to the rule of law in Canada? Why has order given way to force, tension and fear? Why has armed confrontation replaced the peace and natural routine of ordinary daily life?

Consider the ways in which we have settled differences. First, there was the rule of force. Physical might and brute force prevailed. Then as civilized peoples we progressed to the rule of law. Now, we observe struggles for the rule of legitimacy.

We are moving into an era that will see more of us involved in some form of open conflict—a time when Canadian leadership will be challenged to invent and support new approaches to political decision-making and conflict resolution within society. We see evidence of this almost daily: there is

72

increasing pressure from people to participate fully in matters of importance to them—yet our processes of political participation and our methods of dispute resolution lag behind the challenges.

The tragedy is that groups who seek the rule of legitimacy are often frustrated by existing administrative processes and by the adversarial, costly and time-consuming features of courts. In the face of this, frustrated people—like the Mohawks at Oka—are often reduced themselves to using the rule of force. And we have already confirmed among ourselves that force is not desirable—that even where it appears to work, it only establishes a type of "order", but certainly not peace.

We need conflict resolution processes that can be offered to disputing parties long before the conflict escalates to violence. We need to develop skills in resolving disputes through effective negotiation and the many forms of assisted negotiation—among them fact-finding and the facilitation of problem-solving by an independent third party, mediation, and multi-party consensus building techniques—and binding arbitration when the parties wish it.

Imposed settlements are becoming less and less acceptable to people in conflict. Both the process used to settle the dispute and the settlement itself must be legitimate: the process and the outcome must be acceptable to the parties involved, and must be designed to produce a resolution of the conflict.

Oka, for example, was much more than a dispute over the golf course land. Yes, the land claim of the Mohawks, originally made some 15 years ago to the federal government, must be resolved. Deeper still is the issue of self-determination and the legitimate participation of Native people in matters of fundamental importance to them.

Just as Aboriginal people will find the power to assert themselves, so too will others. In fact, as one group presses for its fair share of the pie, others who perceive that this will result in less for them will also press. "Power to the people" is more than a slogan: it points to the urgent need for dispute resolution approaches that will not cause us to regress to violence; it calls for inclusive processes so that push will not become shove. This is the challenge, the need for a fundamental shift.

The Solution:
It's time for a new life science

Conflict has been with us since the dawning of civilization and it will always be with us. Conflict can be beneficial, breaking stagnation and stimulating necessary change. The disabling and destructive effects of poorly managed conflict are also well known.

It has been stated that there are five basic means by which we can manage conflict: we can avoid it, withdraw from it; use coercion; be violent, or choose to negotiate settlements to our disputes and disagreements.

Avoidance and withdrawal may be very effective in certain types of conflict situations or at specific points within a given dispute. For example, a break in negotiations when things become heated is often the best way of ensuring that progress toward solutions may be made; a retreat from a potentially violent outbreak in a family dispute is preferable by far to abuse and violence.

Asian cultures tend to emphasize conflict avoidance as a preferred conflict management technique, and for these people, adversarial approaches, including litigation, are the alternative to avoidance, accommodation and negotiation.

In Western cultures we tend to emphasize the individual and have respect for those who will stand up for themselves. A "Rambo" mentality is part of our popular culture.

Little actual training in negotiation and problem solving is given to our children and the role models they have are adults who are not better off. The distinctions between being assertive and being aggressive are unclear for many people; and the skills of assertiveness and anger management are usually provided only to those people who are thought to "have a problem".

If we are unable to solve interpersonal problems in the home and on the job, we have much to learn about ourselves. A new life science must include a balance of feminine and masculine attributes in each of us and constructive conflict management skills. We need to learn how to get along together more productively, more creatively, and more happily. We need to learn how to live with our differences.

When most of our natural resources are still at relatively high levels and yet we are unable to resolve how we will harvest and distribute them effectively to reduce poverty and

74

starvation and ensure sustainable development, we have great challenges ahead of us.

A life science that embraces and builds upon the strengths of win-win competitiveness will help us make sense of the dramatic changes we are encountering. While life might be chaotic, we should have a set of attitudes and practical skills that would give us a sense of reliability in our personal, employment and social relations. The *whole* human being must be considered in new work arrangements.

Adults should be assertive without being aggressive; collaborative problem solving approaches would replace arbitrary authoritarian and punitive models in our schools; our notions of productivity and worker responsibility would reflect an understanding of the needs and abilities of the total human being; and people would take on new roles and responses to the disputes they encounter.

We are reminded each day that we are in a evolutionary stage as old patterns and standards no longer apply. Win-Win Competitiveness is part of an evolutionary step in our social technology.

SECTION IV

A National Strategy

Re-Tooling for Win-Win Competitiveness in Canada: A National Strategy for Success

Overview

Canadian business and the Canadian public are exhausted by the strains and changes that have assaulted them in the past decade. The rejection of the Charlottetown Accord was, perhaps, the greatest single declaration by Canadians that they have had enough. So strong a repudiation of an agreement that enjoyed the unanimous support of political leaders of all stripes is fundamentally disturbing. The lack of confidence in elected leaders, and the general sense that a vision for Canada has not been expressed by anyone leaves Canada in the lurch.

As Canadians we tend as well to reject any systems of "true belief", and any prophets. We wish for a strong country and insist on respect for regional autonomy. We expect to go first class, and are naive about the economics that are necessary to support such an appetite. We are ambivalent about competitiveness, and we are anxious about our ability to meet the challenges of a global economy that seems inconsiderate of our values and social sensibilities. It bothers us that money does not respect borders and that the pursuit of profit will determine so many things.

We claim a special place in the world as a "mediator" and as "peacekeepers", but we are actually quite parochial and uncomfortable with genuine cultural and ethnic diversity.

We tend to distance ourselves from the values and behaviour of our American neighbours, yet we look to them for economic salvation and we mimic their pop culture.

Isn't it time to do our own thing?

What could we do that would not offend the best of who and what we are and that will take us where we need and want to go?

One course of action is to develop our Win-Win Competitiveness.

To do so, you can start anywhere, right where you are. No gurus, no particular leader, no political party, and no religious or cultural ideology or program are necessary. You can implement consensus-based approaches now in whatever area you choose.

Areas to Work On

On a national level, major strides can be taken to enhance Canadian win-win competitiveness, some of which are the following:

Management-labour relations

In order to improve productivity in the workplace, good relations between Management and Labour are necessary.

The skills, tools and systems of conflict resolution, conflict analysis and conflict prevention are available and must be adapted to each workplace. Respect for cultural diversity and adherence to the principles of human rights and equality are virtues and strengths in the workplace. In an increasingly multicultural Canada, and a global village, diversity is a fact of life, and the ability of business to function effectively in a multicultural reality is essential.

The inherently adversarial nature of management-employee relations works against the objective of win-win competitiveness. Where management and labour wish to bridge the gap by implementing employee ownership schemes or less radical innovations, every effort to do so should be supported by all involved.

Innovation in this direction includes the wave of enthusiasm lead by Peter's "pursuit of excellence" trend which took off in the 80s, and the attempts to transplant Japanese styles of management and the organization of production into industry in the mid-80s.

Continuous Quality Improvement programs, Total Quality Management, and active Employee Relations Committees are efforts that have met with some success. We argue in favour of a made-in-Canada approach and we believe that nothing short of radical change will suffice.

Government

Governments in Canada will need to build systems that facilitate business and commercial problem-solving, the development of smart regulations that are understood by industry and are enforceable, preferably through voluntary compliance; and financial investment in programs that educate and train people in win-win approaches and non-adversarial systems for dispute resolution, both private-commercial and public.

Analysis of conflict

Greater knowledge and skill in the analysis of conflict will need to be developed.

Thus, operational questions for *parties in authority*, say an environmental regulations enforcement agency dealing with a chemical producing factory that is alleged to be pumping toxic wastes into a near-by river, must be capable of appropriate case selection for negotiated rather than punitive approaches; and for problem analysis, strategy development, and enforceability of decisions.

Likewise, *private sector firms* must understand the motivations of competitors, of the other side in a negotiation, and be able to estimate accurately the probability of a consensus-based solution to issues that special interest groups and concerned public are increasingly bringing into play, and affecting private sector plans and bottom lines. When do we meet them face-to-face, should we negotiate, what is really at play here, when is it wise to take the matter to a court of higher appeal? Can a solution be found in a much more creative way than we are now proceeding?

Organizations will have to develop operational guidelines and procedures to address a variety of issues, that if left unattended, could undermine the decisions reached by win-win approaches and precipitate greater problems.

For *government authorities*, these include direction on the role, selection, and appointment of mediators; provisions to meet requirements of public accountability; the use of consensus processes; implementation issues such as linking consensually-derived decisions to institutional capabilities; and measures to protect the final decision-making authority of elected officials when they properly have that prerogative.

For *businesses* these include formation of a customer complaints mechanism, an industry ombudsman, cost-effective mediation and arbitration procedures available to customers and clients, association level responses such as a dispute resolution mechanism available to members, such as insurance or real estate brokers who allege a violation by another member.

Where *public disputes* are concerned, answering the following questions may help government officials determine whether the dispute is suitable for a win-win, consensus-based approach:

‣ is the government fully prepared to disclose the settlement to the public? If not, a consensus-based decision will not meet the need for public accountability.

‣ can the government representative negotiate with sufficient competence to ensure that there is no compromise of departmental standards, significant policy matters, or public rights?

‣ is it necessary to establish a ruling or determine an interpretation of the law? If so, court may be the appropriate forum.

‣ what is the advantage of going to court or using a conventional administrative process, given our relationship with the other party(ies)? Are the transaction costs of trial or of an administrative hearing worth it?

‣ is an acceptable mediator available to mediate this case?

Where a private dispute is the issue, the executives of a business might ask themselves:

Questions to ask in a private dispute

‣ will we be doing business with them again?

‣ how will our approach affect our relationship with them or others in the business community who are important to us?

‣ what is the cost of fighting compared to negotiating?

‣ are we likely to "win" if we fight them in the court, or in some adversarial forum available to us?

‣ are there any costs associated with "winning"

‣ what is our best alternative to an agreement we might negotiate with them?

‣ do we have people who can take a win-win approach here, and build consensus?

81

> what do we do if we can't find a win-win solution with them?

Social relations

A long-term effort to transform our social relations will need to start immediately: by changing the role of education in society and the way in which educators teach collaboration and exercise their authority; by instilling a vision in people as private citizens and professionals to undertake their own self-development in conflict resolution skills so that we steadily educate and train ourselves for peace; by giving communities the incentives and structures to build and be rewarded for both formal and informal economies, including voluntarism, a collaborative activity which adds greatly to the quality of our lives but currently is not integrated into our economic thinking.

Education

1. The federal and provincial governments should invest heavily in education. Starting at the elementary level, students should be taught:
   > critical thinking
   > problem solving
   > learning; that is, how we learn and how to learn
   > anger management and assertiveness
   > religions and cultures of the world
   > languages
   > financial management and investment

2. Apprenticeship programs should be a fundamental element of the educational process. Success in co-operative

82

programs involving the private sector in the education and development of students should be expanded. Such programs should take place across the spectrum of employment opportunities and they should start earlier in the student's development. The long-term goal is to bring the private sector in Canada and the educational system into a partnership in the education, training and development of young people.

3. So that we are able to be leaders in the international community, and competitive in the global marketplace, all Canadians should one day be able to speak two or more languages. In addition to our concentration on English and French, other languages should include Spanish, Japanese, Chinese and those languages which are projected to be the most popular and important in international relations.

4. Emerging centres in Canada which are non-governmental and are advancing the knowledge about and use of alternative forms of conflict resolution should be supported by the relevant government authorities. We need to develop, test, refine and advance the use of dispute resolution across the spectrum of Canadian social, business and public relations.

Trade and Commerce

5. All interprovincial trade barriers in Canada must be eliminated. An independently provided, federally and provincially supported Alternative Dispute Resolution service, including mediation and arbitration, should be set up to facilitate the resolution of any interprovincial trade disputes.

6. Building on models such as the British Columbia International Commercial Arbitration Centre (BCICAC), Canada should establish in concert with other countries, centres for international commercial dispute resolution. Canadian businesses should feel confident that they are able to work in foreign countries with the assurance that any problem or dispute which may arise will be dealt with quickly and cost-effectively. Businesses in other countries should know that Canada has such problem-solving and dispute resolution mechanisms in place.

Employment

7. Perforations in the line between management and labour should continue to be expanded. Innovations such as joint ownership schemes, rotation of workers through different levels of responsibility, team building and consensus approaches, employee complaints and suggestion procedures, and preventative mediation programs should all be encouraged with a view to eroding any destructive divisions in the Canadian workplace.

8. It is time that the informal economy be recognized and integrated into Canadian economic and socio-political thinking. The "Informal Economy", which includes barter, community-based development initiatives, cooperative forms of financing and commercial activity, and voluntarism is a critical element in the health and welfare of the economy. It will be increasingly relevant in a post-industrial world which simply does not require all the available labour power to drive the industrial machine. The volume of "voluntary" contribution to the community must be recognized, rewarded, and expanded.

9. All unemployment insurance schemes should have three elements: job search; community service; training and development. No one should be paid to stay at home or to do nothing. Each third of the program can be planned for individual recipients so that an unemployed person is active in community service for a portion of his/her time; active in skills development; and active in job search. The objective is development of the whole person to support a sense of dignity and self-worth through what can be a very discouraging period. For those who wish to become independently self-employed, financial and business programs should be made available.

Dispute Resolution

10. The federal and provincial governments should adopt dispute resolution legislation similar to that passed into law in the USA in 1990. In 1990, two acts to encourage and strengthen cost-effective dispute resolution in the USA

include the Administrative Dispute Resolution Act, and the Regulatory Negotiation Act.

11. The Canadian National Roundtable on the Economy and the Environment, and its provincial counterparts should assert a leadership role in developing, testing, and expanding the use of non-adversarial procedures and techniques for the resolution of environmental disputes. The dilemma of "Jobs versus Trees" must be overcome; sustainable development must be a workable concept.

12. Consensus-based political decision-making processes, and non-adversarial forms of resolving public policy impasses should be identified and adapted for implementation at all levels of the political decision-making system in Canada.

Tools to Help You Get Started Now

CHAPTER THIRTEEN

The Win-Win Competitiveness Toolbox

An Overview of Conflict Resolution

To implement Win-Win Competitiveness it is helpful to have an overview in the field of conflict resolution. To build your competitiveness using win-win approaches requires "architectural drawings", material, and tools. The architectural drawings are the overview, the materials are the people you rely on and the tools are in the tool box for your selection and use.

What is conflict?

‣ Conflict is the perception of incompatible interests.
‣ Conflict can be both constructive or destructive
‣ Conflict is a process with dimensions and levels; interventions leading to resolution are possible at all levels.
‣ Rarely is conflict "zero-sum", where a "win" for one party necessarily means a "loss" for the other.
‣ The overall relationship among participants in a dispute is very important to its successful resolution; rarely do conflicts occur one time only.

Value of conflict

‣ Effective individuals are not preoccupied with eliminating all forms of resistance. Conflict provides an opportunity to explore issues, develop alternatives and build commitment.

‣ Conflict may raise the level of motivation and energy available to perform required tasks.

‣ A greater diversity of viewpoints may encourage highly creative responses to the heightened sense of the need to resolve a given issue.

‣ The process of articulating a particular viewpoint helps people develop a capacity for analytical problem solving.

Sources of conflict

‣ Objective sources are primarily rational or factual. Conflict can arise from:
  - the diversity of information available to parties
  - a lack of clarity of problems and objectives
  - competition for scarce resources
  - differences in methods and procedures

‣ Subjective sources are primarily emotional or psychological. Conflict can arise from:
  - differing assumptions and perceptions
  - individual needs and goals
  - an individual's communication or influence style

Conflict and current trends

‣ There is a growing tendency for individual and special interest groups to assert their interests through our legal and political systems. Conflict is becoming more "open" in Canada.

‣ Traditional conflict mediating institutions (the family, religious institutions, and the community) are strained in many societies, placing pressure upon governments to establish new means of managing conflicts and of resolving disputes.

‣ More and more business and commercial operations must operate in the context of international trade agreements and the political and social conditions of other countries. Value systems and business practices often clash and competition is increasing.

‣ There is a growing global awareness of the importance of the protection of the environment to the survival and enhancement of human life. Social values place restraints on activities.

89

Education and the conflict

▸ Many basic conflict management skills and techniques, including negotiation and mediation, can be learned in actual or simulated disputes.

▸ Conflict resolution professionals have specialized training in conflict analysis, negotiation and dispute resolution from recognized programs, such as British Columbia Justice Institute and the Canadian International Institute of Applied Negotiation. Their skills have been developed in applying techniques, such as negotiation, mediation, facilitation and fact-finding to a variety of commercial and public disputes.

▸ Significant influences in conflict resolution have come from communications, organization development, program planning and evaluation, and conflict analysis, including alternative dispute resolution (ADR).

Major Criticisms of Traditional Systems of Dispute Resolution

Adversarial nature

▸ The adversarial nature of the legal system, both within the courts and between lawyers, means money is spent on the process of "winning" rather than finding "solutions" that meet the interests of both parties.

▸ The adversarial nature of proceedings disrupts, sometimes destroys, continuing relations between parties.

▸ Court decisions may channel resources to preparation for further legal action rather than preventative problem-solving.

Process

▸ About 90% of all cases are settled before reaching the trial stage. The negotiated outcomes in many cases, however, come very late in the day and may not provide the best solutions to the conflicts.

▸ The pressure of deadlines and the use of adversarial techniques may mean that the outcome is not fair, efficient, stable or wise for either party.

▸ Courts are not the best forum for resolving some disputes:

90

- judges may lack expertise in the subject matter of the dispute
- courts operate within rigid rules and guidelines that may obscure the genuine issues between parties and restrict creative solutions.

Cost and delay

‣ High costs are incurred due to:
- the complexity of the legal system which necessitates employing highly paid professionals
- the lack of timely resolution of disputes which may disrupt the business of the parties and increase legal costs.

Major Advantages of Alternative Dispute Resolution

Choice and control

‣ The consensual nature of the process means parties have control from initiation through to resolution of the dispute. They can walk away at any time.
‣ The parties can choose between different conflict resolution techniques and levels of expertise best suited to resolving the particular conflict.
‣ The parties can retain legal counsel to ensure their rights are not being violated in an alternative forum.

Process

‣ The parties make decisions about the process based on:
- the complexity of the dispute
- the nature of the issues
- the amount of resources in time and money that will be committed to the dispute
- the level of expertise required to settle the dispute
‣ The parties decide on the techniques to be used:
- unassisted negotiation (direct face-to-face)
- assisted negotiation: fact-finding, facilitation, mediation, mini-trial
‣ Considerations regarding the structure and formality of the process:
- prior to the session: the amount of analysis required

91

- during the session: the length, deadlines, scheduling and agenda
- the outcome: binding or non-binding agreements, written or verbal agreements, ratification by parties not at the table

Level of expertise

‣ Unassisted Negotiation: The parties, or their representatives, work it out between themselves, preferably using some basic skills and techniques
‣ Assisted Negotiation: a neutral third party assists the parties
  - Facilitator: assists with the process and not substantive issues
  - Mediator: assists with the process and substantive issues

Costs

‣ Compared to litigation, conflict resolution is a more cost-effective way to settle disputes. Some estimates are that it is 10% to 20% of the cost of litigation.
‣ Research shows that agreements reached through conflict resolution techniques, such as mediation, have a high rate of compliance.
‣ Costs depend on the complexity of the dispute and the level of expertise required.

Inside the Tool-Box

THE FIRST ESSENTIAL:
Conflict resolution skills

 What are conflict resolution skills? Are they any different than the skills we each use every day? Doesn't it all boil down to being a good communicator?

No. There is more to it than that.

Conflict resolution skills are not something we are born with. We acquire our fundamental values and attitudes from others, usually long before we have anything to say about it, and we repeat and practice the conflict resolution skills of those who have influenced us most in our development.

In the course of a normal day, no matter who you are and what role you play, you will be confronted by conflict situations. You may actually advance a cause or confront someone so that you are seen as the source of the conflict. Conflict is normal, and as already noted it may be destructive or constructive. Conflict motivates some people and it depresses and literally immobilizes others.

We choose various conflict management approaches, with some effectiveness. Depending on the circumstances, and our skills, we may choose to withdraw from a conflict, to avoid a conflict, to manipulate and coerce those with whom we are in conflict, and in certain cases, we act violently.

The choice of skills we use depends to some extent on our attitudes toward conflict, as we have already outlined. Manipulation, coercion, and violence are clearly not conflict resolution skills; they may control and repress the expression of the conflict for a time, but they will not produce a resolution, let alone a heart-felt settlement that the underdog will be content to live with.

Within the negotiation option, the preferred choice for managing conflicts, it is also the case that styles of negotiation will vary and the skills may include accommodating or yielding, compromise, trade-offs and various bargaining behaviours.

Conflict resolution skills, no matter how well trained and practised, are of limited value in circumstances that call for sound conflict analysis, or when the environment simply will not support their use. The tools of conflict analysis are necessary to be certain the right skills are being used at the right time; and systems, or a social technological infrastructure are required to support analysis and the application of skills.

Some conflict resolution skills

› active listening
› anger management, including self-control and assertiveness
› problem solving, including linear and lateral thinking
› communication in various forms and for various audiences
› ability to analyze conflict
› negotiation skills, the art and science of persuasion
› facilitation skills, both in small and large groups
› ability to evaluate, and assess objectively
› conciliation techniques, including fact finding
› mediation skills, including trust building, patience and humour

93

> ▸ ability to analyze individual and group motivation and behaviour
> ▸ participatory leadership skills
> ▸ team building

Description of Conflict Resolution Techniques

NEGOTIATION ➔
    FACILITATION ➔
        MEDIATION ➔
            FACT FINDING ➔
                MINI-TRIAL ➔
                    ARBITRATION

Negotiation

By far the most commonly used alternative to trial is negotiation. Research in Canada and the United States confirms that 90% of cases are settled by negotiation between counsel prior to trial.

Negotiation itself is treated as both an art and a science. Centres such as the Program on Negotiation at the Harvard Law School and the Canadian International Institute of Applied Negotiation teach "principled negotiation" or "negotiating on the merits"; the interests of the parties are important in addition to industry standards and alternatives available away from the table.

Facilitation

Facilitation is the simplest form of assisted negotiation. A third party helps disputants to negotiate a settlement, focusing almost entirely on the process.

Facilitators may act as moderators, especially when there are more than two disputants. As moderators they monitor the quality of the dialogue, offering questions or prompts intended to enhance communication and understanding between the disputants. Facilitators seldom address substantive issues in the dispute. Their emphasis is on communication, using whatever tools are available to create and maintain an environment conducive to joint problem solving.

Facilitation is preferred by disputants who may primarily want assistance with the process only, without intervention at the substantive level of their dispute.

Mediation

Mediation is a structured process where an impartial and neutral third party without decision-making power assists parties to settle their differences through negotiation. Mediation, like Facilitation, is a form of assisted negotiation, although mediation intensifies the substantive involvement of the neutral. Mediation is especially appropriate as an alternative means of dispute resolution when conflicts have hardened and communication has broken down.

Mediators often meet privately with the parties prior to the mediation session to determine their interests and possible substantive trades. Mediators take an active role in discussions. They may convene private caucuses with the parties during the face-to-face negotiation sessions to explore room for movement, to clarify issues or to determine the points of resistance to resolution. Mediators have no authority over the outcome, they have no right to impose a resolution, and they must respect the parties' agreement, reflecting the disputants' sense of what is acceptable and what represents success.

Mediators must have the trust and confidence of the disputants, enabling them to convene and facilitate the negotiation, to create a collaborative problem-solving atmosphere, and to offer ideas that may reflect a consensus and form the basis of a settlement. Participation in mediation, as in all consensual processes, is voluntary although some jurisdictions invite mediation as a mandatory step in the dispute resolution process made available to disputants. Voluntary participation includes:

‣ control over the decision to participate, veto power over the choice of the mediator and over the process;
‣ direct input into settling the agenda
‣ being able to walk away at any time; and
‣ deciding whether the agreements negotiated in mediation are binding or non-binding.

Fact finding

Parties in dispute may choose to jointly engage in Fact Finding as a step in negotiating a settlement, whether they

95

are negotiating directly without assistance, or are participating in some form of assisted negotiation. In the context of Alternative Dispute Resolution, Fact Finding is one of a number of consensual processes, to be distinguished from the partisan presentation of evidence, including expert testimony, in the context of adversarial proceedings. Fact Finding jointly commissioned by the disputants, most likely on the recommendation of a Facilitator or Mediator, and serving as a neutrally executed act, is most certainly a common element of assisted negotiation.

Mini-trial

The Mini-trial is not a trial but a voluntary forum designed to assist principals in a dispute negotiate a settlement. Each side chooses a senior person usually not involved in the emotional aspects of the dispute. Then a mutually acceptable third party is selected to preside at the hearing or "trial". Lawyers for both sides present their best case to the principals and the neutral, who may ask questions. Then the principals, with the assistance of the neutral, try to negotiate a settlement. If an agreement cannot be reached, none of the information shared during the mini-trial may be used as evidence during subsequent proceedings. Mini-trials were privately developed to help bring about negotiated settlement instead of corporate litigation.

Mini-trials may be used between private parties, completely outside the courts, and they are a form of conflict resolution that seems particularly well-suited to certain government disputes, such as contract disputes.

Arbitration

There are several types of Arbitration. These include private commercial, international commercial, labour (for both grievance and collective bargaining disputes) and various forms of court-ordered arbitration.

Arbitration is generally described as a dispute resolution process for contract disputes in which disputants present proofs and arguments to a neutral third party who has the authority to hand down a binding decision, generally based on objective standards. In Last Offer Arbitration the arbitrator is required to choose between the final positions of the two parties.

The authority for decision-making may be handed over voluntarily by the parties in advance of the proceeding as in the case of a completely private commercial dispute, or the arbitrator's authority may be mandated by the court.

The setting for arbitration is usually more formal than that for consensual processes but the procedure is less formal, less complex and often concluded more quickly than court proceedings.

THE SECOND ESSENTIAL:
Tools for conflict analysis

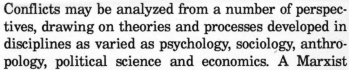

Conflicts may be analyzed from a number of perspectives, drawing on theories and processes developed in disciplines as varied as psychology, sociology, anthropology, political science and economics. A Marxist dialectical analysis of power and class structures, a sociometric analysis of group dynamics or a cross-cultural analysis of the role of cultural identity in race conflicts are each valid depending on the situation.

A combination of approaches is most realistic, as evidenced in the increasing emphasis in most disciplines towards a multi-disciplinary, holistic and a systems view. The analyst of conflict, whether a professional in the field of conflict resolution, a negotiator facing her next deal, or a production manager on the factory floor looking for solutions to problems, will want a varied repertoire.

Conflict analysis tools include:

Forms of Conflict Management

Assessing which general form of conflict management is being used by the participants in the conflict:

‣ Avoidance
‣ Withdrawal
‣ Coercion
‣ Violence
‣ Negotiation

Three Essential Elements of Conflict Resolution

Assessing to what extent the three essential elements of conflict resolution are evident and/or utilized by the participants (Skills; Tools; Systems or an infrastructure for successful conflict management):

97

> Skills
> Tools
> Systems

Roles

Assessing which role the individuals in the conflict tend to play or opt for under stress:
> Activist
> Advocate
> Mediator
> Researcher/Observer
> Enforcer

Galtung's Conflict Management Triangle

Using Galtung's Conflict Management Triangle to diagnose the problem (Conflict situation; Conflict Attitudes; Conflict Behaviour —is this a situation that generates incompatible goals or values among different parties; are there psychological and cognitive processes that appear to engender

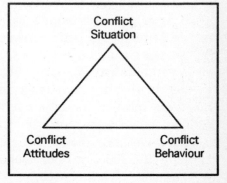

conflict or are consequent to it; are actual, observed activities undertaken by one party and designed to injure, thwart or eliminate the opponent):

Circle Chart

Using the Circle Chart, designed by Professor Roger Fisher and William Ury and presented in *Getting to Yes*, to determine:

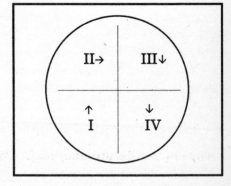

I   the current symptoms;
II   a diagnosis by sorting the symptoms to determine causes;

III developing possible strategies or prescriptions, including broad ideas about action, or theoretical cures; and
IV identifying specific steps to deal with the problem.

Force Field Analysis

Using a Force Field analysis to identify all forces working against resolution of the conflict, and all forces supporting resolution of the conflict, then designing a strategy to orchestrate the forces supporting resolution and to neutralize or convert the forces against resolution:

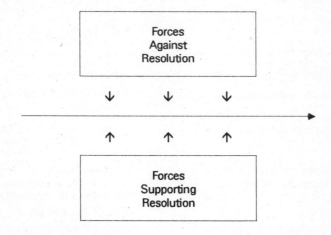

Seven Elements

Examining the conflict, or state of dissensus from the perspective of seven elements identified by Professor Fisher and his colleagues at Harvard as the essential ingredients in building consensus (what are the parties' **alternatives**—choices available to them away from the table; what are the parties' underlying **interests**—their needs, concerns, wants and fears; what kind of **communication**—verbal and nonverbal/serving informational needs and emotional needs—is being used and is it effective; what are the **standards of legitimacy**—or objective criteria, such as case law, precedents, industry standards —that are or may be used to settle the problem on its merits; what is the nature and quality of the **relationship**—the level of trust, familiarity, rapport, history and potential—between the parties and how is it affecting the conflict and the possible resolution; what are the **options**—creative solutions and

99

packages which respond to interests—available for resolution; what is the role of **commitment** here—including the degree of commitment the parties have to finding a resolution to the problem and their willingness and ability to honour any commitments they make):

▸ Alternatives
▸ Interests
▸ Communication
▸ Standards of Legitimacy
▸ Relationship
▸ Options
▸ Commitment

Costs and Benefits

Assessing the conflict situation to determine the benefits and costs associated, and to whom these are allocated:

ON THE BENEFITS SIDE, DETERMINE:	ON THE COSTS SIDE, DETERMINE:
▸ whether the conflict has an Equalizing effect— putting parties on an equal footing;	▸ whether the conflict is or will likely result in conquest, elimination or annihilation of one of the parties;
▸ an Attention-arresting effect— focusing attention on the real problem in the circumstance;	▸ whether the use of avoidance or withdrawal are entailing costs and damages; and
▸ a Solidifying effect—increasing the internal cohesion of an individual psychological and spiritual being or that of a group or organization's;	▸ whether or not cycles of violence or vengeance are likely to ensue from the manner in which the conflict is being managed.
▸ a Preventative effect, with respect to social stagnation; —the effect of Encouraging growth and change of individuals, groups or organizations;	
▸ whether the conflict is Stimulating innovation; and	
▸ whether the conflict is Functioning as a "safety valve" for the individual, group, organization or system, overall.	

THE THIRD ESSENTIAL:
Systems for conflict prevention

 Our skills in conflict resolution are actually under-developed. Rhetoric within mainstream Western society is that individuals, groups and organizations will be rewarded for demonstrating a set of skills that are diametrically opposed to conflict resolution. We are not only to "speak up" and "stand up" for ourselves; we are to "kick butt"; we are to strive, achieve, dominate and win. The Rambo mentality is alive and well.

Some of the costs associated with this mythology, ideology, and rhetoric have been discussed here and each of us has our own personal accounts of the strengths and weaknesses of a life led in that way.

We know as well, that it simply is not the case that the promises and implied victories and rewards of this approach to life really pan out for the majority. *There is an increasing sense that fewer and fewer are enjoying the "winnings".*

We also fail to separate the value of asserting ourselves in defence and support of our legitimate interests, needs and concerns from the rhetoric of dominance and victory through aggression and predatory behaviour. Conflict resolution skills will demand strength, fortitude, and the controlled and constructive use of power. But this is different than the abuse of power in the service of beating the other side. A person skilled in conflict resolution must understand power and must know *"what" to do and "when to do it"* to effect a resolution.

Even with the best skills, we still require the faculty and tools of analysis to ensure proper application.

The systems for conflict prevention are even less developed, despite some remarkably successful innovations, and despite the piece-meal efforts throughout North America to build alternatives for people who wish to solve problems more effectively, and to manage conflict more constructively, whether in the community or in the corporate boardroom.

The idea of "systems of conflict prevention" is itself the subject of some controversy. Clearly, given the benefits that conflict may have, some would say it is not even desirable to prevent it. Perhaps an more accurate term to describe what is intended here by the term conflict prevention is conflict "remediation". The idea being to remedy a conflict situation, to solve it, before it escalates, as conflicts are prone to do.

101

The application of conflict resolution skills based on sound analysis will of course be remedial, if successful. The conflict, properly managed, may generate considerable benefits with little cost, and it will be settled or resolved. *Strictly speaking, therefore, pure conflict prevention would thus be lost opportunity.* For while the costs would be prevented, so would the benefits. Conflict is necessary, even desirable.

The use of the term prevention, however, remains helpful to underline the need for policies, procedures, and mechanisms that support the skills and tools that make Win-Win Competitiveness possible.

In essence, a social infrastructure must be built to support win-win competitiveness. In some cases, say the appointment of an ombudsman or the availability of a employee complaint system in a workplace, the conflict resolution system may "prevent" a conflict. It will more likely ensure that there are readily available means in organizations, in society, in government, and in the legal apparatus to exploit win-win approaches.

Some policies, procedures and mechanisms for conflict prevention are:

▸ Ombudsman: An ombudsman (whether within a corporation or at the provincial or federal levels, empowered to investigate complaints that are not being resolved through normal channels and with the authority to recommend changes that will prevent conflicts).

▸ Non-adversarial Boards: Various quasi-judicial panels and tribunals, especially those that are expanding their use of non-adversarial proceedings and techniques to solve problems, make recommendations and settle disputes promptly.

▸ ADR Legislation: Legislation supporting the appointment of mediators, neutral evaluators, fact finders to intervene in disputes and in the context of what might otherwise be lengthy and cumbersome administrative and bureaucratic processes.

▸ Employee Suggestions: A number of employee complaint or suggestion procedures.

▸ Customer Dispute Resolution Mechanisms: Customer dispute mediation or arbitration mechanisms.

‣ Preventative Mediation Programs: Preventative mediation programs to deal with many items of interest to management and labour but which are often not addressed in standard labour relations practices or collective bargaining sessions.

‣ Conflict Resolution Component in EAPs: Employee assistance programs that include a conflict resolution component in addition to assessment and referral for individual needs such as stress and alcohol abuse counselling, financial management coaching and family therapy.

‣ Mediation of Sexual Harassment: Sexual harassment policies and procedures for remediation.

‣ Student Peer Mediation: Student peer mediation programs in schools and on campuses.

‣ International Dispute Resolution: International dispute resolution bodies such as the International Joint Commission, formed to settle disputes that arise along the Canada-US border.

‣ Model Mediation/Arbitration Clause: **All disputes arising out of, or in connection with, this Agreement/ Contract or in respect of any defined legal relationship associated therewith or derive therefrom, shall be referred to mediation/arbitration.**

CHAPTER FOURTEEN

Working Assumptions Behind Win-Win Competitiveness

▸ The definition of "competitive" used here is: "depending for effectiveness on the relative concentration of two or more substances"

▸ In individuals, and in societies, there is a tension between a drive to compete and a drive to cooperate.

▸ Competition can be healthy.

▸ Cooperation often produces better outcomes than competition: (Collaboration often produces better outcomes than noncollaboration, i.e., two heads are often better than one).

▸ Choosing a competitive mode or a cooperative mode to the exclusion of the other is a counter-productive strategy in a complex world where there is a demand for both competitive and cooperative initiatives; often at the same time.

▸ In two-party and even multi-party bargaining situations there exists the opportunity to collaborate to produce options that meet the interests of the parties resulting in joint gains *or* to expand the pie to enhance the probability of meeting the competitive interests of the parties (i.e., satisfying each individual's particular interests).

▸ In an organizational context, strictly adversarial approaches to management-employee relations or, externally, to other organizations (even competitors) fail to realize the advantages to be found in the constructive management of the tension between competitive drives and cooperative/collaborative approaches.

‣ Relationships that are more than single episode relationships (encounters) tend to be complex and interdependent; complex, interdependent relationships require new attitudes with respect to power, communication and modes of relating.

‣ Complex interdependent relationships between individuals, within organizations, and between organizations render win-lose approaches inappropriate and, practically speaking, counterproductive.

‣ Win-win approaches do not imply a sacrifice of fundamental principles or a compromise of the legitimate interests and needs of the parties. In practical organizational or business terms this implies that employees' interests cannot be sacrificed in the interests of management; that is, employees' interest for proper remuneration, reliable terms and conditions of employment, and opportunity for input and participation in the decision-making process. Similarly for managers and employers: their interest for appropriate return on investment, the exercise of managerial discretion in overall mission and objectives of the firm cannot be sacrificed.

‣ Win-Win Competitiveness implies the collaborative approach to all sub-sets of human relations and business activities in the service of enhancing individual and organizational productivity and effectiveness thereby contributing directly to the health and morale of individuals and relationships, and the competitiveness of business.

‣ At the practical level this can be seen in internal matters with respect to employer-employee relationships, in marketing approaches, in sales and the closing of contracts, in the external relations of the firm with suppliers and clients, and even in the collaboration between competitor firms in the form of strategic alliances, joint ventures, and mergers to ensure productivity, effectiveness, and survival.

‣ Win-Win Competitiveness places competition four-square and builds upon recent developments in the field of negotiation advanced by Roger Fisher, Harvard Law School, David Lax and James Sebenius and their colleagues in

105

their leading work on "principled negotiation" or "negotiating on the merits".

‣ Win-Win Competitiveness recognizes the inherent adversarial tendencies or tensions which arise within individuals, within organizations, between individuals and between groups.

‣ Win-Win Competitiveness is Canadian in character in that it reflects the essential Canadian tendency to enjoy and express fully the competitive drives of people and at the same time to strive for collaboration and win-win solutions to problems. Neither the individual nor the collective dominates. Neither is sacrificed or reduced in a melting pot.

Moving Forward

THERE are plenty of "how to" books that promise to teach the reader how to win by being more competitive. The central idea in this book is how to be more competitive by using the win-win approach.

I argue as well that the view in this book is based on our true Canadian character. We should overcome our tendency to look elsewhere for the answer to our problems when we already have what it takes.

Win-Win Competitiveness starts with saying "Canadians are unique and we can build on that. We can distinguish ourselves in the global marketplace by advancing our natural tendencies and our strengths."

People want to live in communities and work in jobs that are not filled with stress and tension. Businesses want to enlist the creative and productive potential of workers. Politicians want to facilitate constructive relations between labour, the private sector and government. Canadians want resolution to Indian land claims. A balance between "jobs" and "trees" must be found.

In this book I have tried to avoid lengthy philosophical arguments and too much theory. Instead, the objective is to give readers a fresh look at our challenges and some ideas about practical "made in Canada" solutions which are available now.

Now it is time for the reader to put Win-Win Competitiveness to the test.

1. The Program on Negotiation at Harvard University has articulated a number of values or working assumptions which underlay the win-win approach to negotiation and dispute resolution. These working assumptions give us more insight into the win-win approach. Some of these are:

   ‣ conflict can be both good or bad, constructive or destructive;
   ‣ conflict is a process, with different dimensions and players;
   ‣ rarely is conflict zero-sum, where a "win" for one party necessarily means a "loss" for the other;
   ‣ if sufficiently resourceful and inventive, negotiators are able to find joint gains in almost any dispute;
   ‣ the techniques of negotiation can be learned;
   ‣ the overall relationship among participants in a dispute is very important to its successful resolution— rarely do conflicts occur between parties one time only.

2. Robert Axelrod's 1984 book, *The Evolution of Cooperation*, explores the nature of cooperation in a world of egoists where no central authority prevails; he examines how cooperation can develop in situations where each individual has an incentive to be selfish. Based on the performance in a computer tournament of a computer program developed by Canadian mathematician, Anatol Rapoport, the author concludes that the evolution of cooperation requires that individuals have a high probability of meeting again so that they have a high stake in their future interaction. The notion of the "shadow of the future" thus becomes influential in our negotiating behaviour. The importance of relationship issues to negotiating strategies and outcomes is underlined.

In his book *The Zero-Sum Society* Lester C. Thurow insists that in our political system every economic decision produces losers and winners; the fact is, our natural resources are in fixed supply, and some are scarce. Thurow sets out both an income distribution scheme and government interventions that will deal with this fundamental fact of life by improving efforts toward achieving the equality being demanded by previously oppressed groups. A large part of Thurow's solution is to be found in better political processes: empowerment through negotiation and consensus-based approaches are implied.

3. See *Breaking the Impasse* by L. Susskind and J. Chruikshank, Basic Books, New York.

4. Fisher and Ury's *Getting to Yes: Reaching Agreement without Giving In*, and Howard Raiffa's *The Art and Science of Negotiation* are particularly relevant. Building on this work, Lax and Sebenius give the reader one of the most simple explanations of the strategic and economic features of win-win approaches. Their book, *The Manager as Negotiator* was seminal to my articulation of win-win competitiveness.

5. Many of us are familiar with Peter's *In Search of Excellence*, and Covey's *Principle Centred Leadership*.

6. We typically associate "competitive" with "American" and overlook our own Competitive tendencies, abilities and successes.

7. The Financial Post, August 31, 1992 editorial "Restructuring puts us in a new ball game" pushes us to look beyond the recession to prepare for a whole new reality in which Canada not only has a place but can play a major role. Our insecurity that Canada is "too small to change economic events" must be put aside in a re-structured international economic order. Quality, not quantity, will be a significant factor in success.

8. In fact, GM's unit Saturn Corp., has been described as the one of the most revolutionary examples of management and labour forming an alliance to achieve joint goals— including survival. In "Forming an uneasy alliance", John

109

Smith, administrative assistant to the president of the United Steelworkers of America is quoted as follows: "An adversarial relationship cannot be compatible with today's market. We're part of a world trade. We're no longer king this and king that". (Associated Press, December 18, 1990).

9. Simpson's article "Training Canada's competitive edge", *Globe and Mail*, February 1, 1991.

10. Roy MacLaren, Liberal MP for Etobicoke North and critic for trade, advocates that we discover a "radical centre", one which "offers a new strategy for sustained growth based on real commitment to equality of opportunity". I believe MacLaren anticipates win-win competitiveness in his "Rediscovering the political 'centre'", *The Financial Post*, March 2, 1992.

11. "Taking Care of Employees", the *Ottawa Citizen*, July 20, 1991.

12. Ibid.

13. Ottawa Citizen, September 12, 1992.

14. Report of the Auditor General of Canada, 1988.

15. See, "Management, labour share in Schneider's success", *Ottawa Citizen*, December, 1991; "Everyone's boss", Associated Press, December 17, 1990; "Forming an uneasy alliance", Associated Press, December 18, 1990; "Teamwork: 'The Secret of Honda's Success'", *Ottawa Citizen*, December 15, 1990; and for a tough account of the limits to skills acquisition and re-organization as the only responses to our competition problems, see "All Quiet on the Factory Floor", the *Globe and Mail*, October 27, 1992.

16. For a helpful discussion of the relationship of OD, TQM, and our focus, ADR, see Ozzie Bermont's "OD, TQM and ADR: The Expanding Universe", in SPIDR *News*, Volume 15, No. 2, Spring 1991. Published by Society of Professionals in Dispute Resolution, Washington, D.C.

17. Business World, April 13, 1992.

18. Paul Weinberg's article in *Law Times*, February 7, 1993, picks up on R. Askov to make a point which is directly in support of my argument. Weinberg's article, "Civil Litigation Backlog blamed on Reluctance of Lawyers to Change" begins "When the Supreme Court of Canada handed down its landmark decision R. Askov in the fall of 1990, it was directing its attention to the sorry state of Ontario's criminal courts. At the time of the ruling *tens of thousands* [emphasis by author] of criminal charges had been outstanding in the province for at least six months and cases were, in some regions, taking well over two years to make to trial."

Weinberg points out just how bad the situation is with respect to civil cases. He cites a real estate dispute that took five years of litigation which could have been settled by mediation. I would suggest this case could have been settled in four hours of mediation in a mediation service similar to the one operated by the Real Estate Board of Ottawa-Carleton.

19. See "Alternative Dispute Resolution: Growth Industry of the '90s", by J.A. Keefe in *Engineering Dimensions*, official Journal, Association of Professional Engineers of Ontario, January/February, 1992.

Selected Readings

Bercovitch, J. 1984. *Social Conflicts and Third Parties*. Boulder Colorado.: Westview Press.

Binnendijk, H. 1987. *National Negotiation Styles*. Washington, D.C.: U.S. Department of State.

Burton, J.W. 1987. *Resolving Deep-Rooted Conflict*. Lanham, Md.: University Press of America.

Carpenter S., and Kennedy, W.J.D. 1988. *Managing Public Disputes: A Practical Guide to Handling Conflict and Reaching Agreements*. San Francisco: Jossey Bass.

Casse, P. and Deol, S. 1985. *Managing Intercultural Negotiations*. Washington, D.C.: Sietar International.

Coser, L. 1956. *The Function of Social Conflict*. Glencoe, Ill.: Free Press.

Covey, S.R. 1990. *Principle-Centred Leadership*. Toronto: Simon & Shuster.

Deutsch, M. 1973. *The Resolution of Conflict*. New Haven, Conn.: Yale University Press.

Fisher, R. and Brown, S. 1988. *Getting Together: Building Relationships As We Negotiate*. Boston: Houghton Mifflin.

Fisher, R. and Ury W. 1981. *Getting to YES: Negotiating Agreements Without Giving In*. Boston: Houghton Mifflin Co.

———. 1978. *International Mediation: A Working Guide*. Cambridge, Mass.: Harvard Negotiation Project.

Henrikson, A.K. 1986. *Negotiating World Order*. Wilmington, Del.: Scholarly Resources.

Hoffman, B. 1990. *Conflict, Power and Persuasion: Negotiating Effectively*. North York, Ont.: Captus Press.

Hofstadter, D.R. 1983. "Metamagical Themas". *Scientific American*, May 1983: 16.

Janosik, R.J. 1987. "Rethinking the Culture-Negotiation Link". *Negotiation Journal* 3 (1987): pp. 385–396.

Kolb, D.M. 1983. *The Mediators*. Cambridge, Mass.: The MIT Press.

Lax, D.A., and Sebenius, J.K. 1986. *The Manager as Negotiator*. New York: The Free Press.

Pruitt, D.G. and Rubin, J.Z. 1986. *Social Conflict: Escalation, Stalemate and Settlement*. New York: Random House.

Raiffa, H. 1982. *The Art and Science of Negotiation*. Cambridge, Mass.: Harvard University Press.

Rubin, J.Z. (Ed.). 1981. *Dynamics of Third Party Intervention*. New York: Praeger Publishers.

Salacuse, J.W. 1991. *Making Global Deals: What Every Executive Should Know About Negotiating Abroad*. Toronto: Random House of Canada.

Sander, F.A.E. 1985. "Alternative Methods of Dispute Resolution: An Overview". *University of Florida Law Review* 37 (1985): pp. 1–18.

Sandole, D.J.D., and Sandole-Staroste, I. 1987. *Conflict Management and Problem Solving: Interpersonal to International Applications*. New York: New York University Press.

Schelling, T. 1960. *The Strategy of Conflict*. Cambridge Mass.: Harvard University Press.

Sunshine, R.B. 1990. *Negotiating for International Development*. Boston: Nijhoff Publishers.

Susskind, L., and Cruikshank, J. 1987. *Breaking the Impasse*. New York: Basic Books.

Touval, S. and Zartman, I.W. (Eds.). 1985. *International Mediation in Theory and Practice*. Boulder Co.: Westview Press.

Walton, R.E. and McKersie, R.B. 1965. *A Behavioral Theory of Labor Negotiations*. New York: McGraw-Hill Book Company.

Weiss, S.E. with Stripp, W. 1985. "Negotiating with Foreign Businesspersons: An Introduction for Americans with Propositions on Six Cultures". New York: New York University Graduate School of Business Administration Working Paper 85-6.